C000173172

Penguin Modern Classics
Friends and Relations

Elizabeth Bowen was born in Dublin in 1899, the only child of an Irish lawyer and landowner. She was educated at Downe House School in Kent. Her book *Bowen's Court* (1942) is the history of her family and their house in County Cork, and *Seven Winters* (1943) contains reminiscences of her Dublin childhood. In 1923 she married Alan Cameron who held an appointment with the BBC and who died in 1952. She travelled a good deal, dividing most of her time between London and Bowen's Court, which she inherited.

She is considered by many to be one of the most distinguished novelists of the present age. She saw the object of a novel as 'the non-poetic statement of a poetic truth' and said that 'no statement of it can be final'. Her first book, *Encounters*, a collection of short stories, appeared in 1923, followed by another, *Ann Lee's*, in 1926. *The Hotel* (1927) was her first novel, and was followed by *The Last September* (1929), *Joining Charles* (1929), another book of short stories, *Friends and Relations* (1931), *To the North* (1932), *The Cat Jumps* (short stories, 1934), *The House in Paris* (1935), *The Death of the Heart* (1938), *Look at All Those Roses* (short stories, 1941), *The Demon Lover* (short stories, 1945), *The Heat of the Day* (1949), *Collected Impressions* (essays, 1950), *The Shelbourne* (1951), *A World of Love* (1955), *A Time in Rome* (1960), *After-thought* (essays, 1962), *The Little Girls* (1964), *A Day in the Dark* (1965) and her last book, *Eva Trout* (1969).

She was awarded the CBE in 1948, and received the honorary degree of Doctor of Letters from Trinity College, Dublin, in 1949 and from Oxford University in 1956. In the same year she was appointed Lacy Martin Donnelly Fellow at Bryn Mawr College in the United States. In 1965 she was made a Companion of Literature by the Royal Society of Literature. Elizabeth Bowen died in 1973.

Elizabeth Bowen

Friends and Relations

Penguin Books

Contents

Part I
Edward and Rodney   7

Part II
The Fine Week   52

Part III
Wednesday   111

TO
B

Part I
Edward and Rodney

I

The morning of the Tilney–Studdart wedding rain fell steadily
from before daylight, veiling trees and garden and darkening the
canvas of the marquee that should have caught the earliest sun in
happy augury. The bride's relations frowned in sleep and were
roused with a sense of doom by rain's inauspicious mutter on roofs
and windowsills. Clouds with their reinforcements came rolling
over the Malvern hills. Till quite late, the rooms at Corunna
Lodge were dusky as though the morning had been delayed.

Laurel Studdart herself was not concerned with weather and
gave the windows hardly a glance. She and Colonel Studdart,
both embarrassed by idleness, frequently met throughout the
morning as, straying from room to room, they attempted to efface
themselves. Her father had the afternoon on his mind – he had not
yet given away a daughter – for her, these hours before her
wedding were like a too long wait on the platform of some familiar
station from which, virtually, one has already departed, where the
very associations become irksome. Her clothes were all packed;
she was buttoned into an old blazer of Janet's and did not look
like today's bride. From half-past ten till noon she and Colonel
Studdart, shut into the morning-room, played demon patience.
Her life here was over, his at a standstill; there was nothing for
them to do. The morning-room flowers had been 'arranged';
freesia banked the fireplace; Colonel Studdart, from nervousness
and a tendency to hay-fever, frequently sneezed. Pollen dashed
Laurel's cheek where she had leant excitedly forward across a
lily.

The rain stopped before lunch. Later, during the ceremony,
the sun came out, parting the clouds widely; so that Laurel's
married way down the aisle was gold from successive windows.
When she uncertainly smiled in the porch, against strong blasts
from the organ rolling out from behind, the umbrellas were finally
down; the graves glittered. It was early-closing day, friends from

7

the Cheltenham shops were among the onlookers. The sweet bride, trailing light in her veil, was nodded and smiled to the car where the chauffeur compromised with his impassivity.

Now the service was over the afternoon steadily brightened. The open-sided marquee was not, after all, to prove a fiasco. Laurel and Edward, obedient to Mrs Studdart's instructions, took up their position in the morning-room. A playing-card, over-looked, lay face down on the carpet. Edward stooped for it – 'Don't!' she cried, 'leave it!' her heart in her mouth. Better not – Finding themselves still alone Edward and she kissed hastily, with a feverish calm. They had all time, but only the moment. Then Laurel arranged her train in a pool, as she had seen brides do. Mrs Studdart, coming in shortly afterwards, re-arranged it.

'You might hold your lilies,' said Mrs Studdart, who had dis-covered the sheaf on a hall table specially cleared for the top-hats.

'Oh, Mother, I *can't*; they're heavy.'

'But don't you think it would be nice, Edward, if she were to hold her lilies?'

'I don't know,' said Edward. 'Do people generally?'

'They'd be such a strain on one arm all the time. You see I can't change them; I must keep my right arm for shaking hands.'

'And shake hands *lightly*,' said Mrs Studdart, 'don't grip.'

'Did I look . . .?'

'Lovely, lovely,' said Mrs Studdart. She was looking round distractedly for a vase and soon found one, a kind of Italian urn in which she arranged the lilies beside the bride.

The house might have been designed for such an occasion. The position of the morning-room was admirable; it had two doors so that the guests could circulate through a chain of rooms. Each, having saluted the bridal pair, was to pass on through the dining-room; through the French window and out by duck-boards into the open-sided marquee. (This was the best of a summer wedding; to make this possible he and she had devoured each other nervously throughout the endless winter of their engagement.) In the dining-room Cousin Richard was to be posted to head the guests off through the window. He would be shot, he said, if he let one past him into the hall.

'I shall depend upon you, Richard,' said Mrs Studdart. (He had been in the Colonies.) 'For if the two streams mix in the hall

8

and people get squeezed back into the drawing-room and have to pass Laurel all over again, there will be the most shocking confusion.'

Janet, the bride's younger sister, knew that Cousin Richard would be certain, sooner or later, to say 'Pass along the car, please.' She supposed that one did not mind? She supposed that someone was bound to be humorous at a wedding? Might not her Wolf Cubs be better? She proffered two. Several had been already allotted to laying down duck-boards or directing cars round the corner where they could park. But Mrs Studdart thought no, on the whole. The little boys' boots ... Besides, one did not want friends to feel like traffic, in any way 'directed'. Also one could not disappoint Cousin Richard, who had been so much in New Zealand.

Janet said: 'Just as you think, of course.'

Young Mr and Mrs Tilney, between her train and the lilies, with a background of pleasant outdoor sunshine, now stood waiting for their photograph by the world to be taken, for the curtain to rise. In the hall, first guests from the church could be heard arriving; Lady Elfrida Tilney tittering in the porch. Their two heads turned, rather beautifully apprehensive; they had an instant for conversation.

Edward: 'This morning, I wanted to ring you up.'

Out of her bride's formality, fall of tulle and lace, came the gay little scoffing laugh. 'Oho!' she remarked.

'But mother kept saying, "*Now* I expect you will ring up Laurel?" So I went out and bought some labels.'

'Labels?'

'For my things.'

'Oh, labels. Well, that's one conversation we'll never have.'

'– They're coming –'

'No, that's the ices going round to the marquee. Edward ...'

But his emotions were quite at a standstill. He had at any time more address than an occasion required. Edward was determined that his wedding, like the execution of Julien Sorel, should go off simply, suitably, without any affectation on his part.

Laurel went on: 'I suppose we can't possibly ...'

But at this point Lady Elfrida brought in the Daubeneys; remarking with the keenest sense of effect: 'My daughter-in-law.' Laurel amazed the Daubeneys with a lovely, composed smile.

9

After the Daubeneys, guests began to come through on a strong current.

Edward remained throughout wonderfully self-possessed; perhaps because of this he did not make an entirely good impression. Lady Elfrida, in claret-coloured georgette, also overacted a little. Besides being a *divorcée*, which should but does not subdue, she was the bridegroom's mother – and one apt to play always a little too gracefully a losing game. The Tilney connection (here to shower on Edward for his marriage as well as his mother a loving depreciation), bright woof to a sober warp, shuttled their way to and fro through the Studdart connection. Impervious to strangers, signalling, smiling, these bright friends distinguished each other; where two or three met intimacies flowered and branched.

In the dining-room, Cousin Richard was more than a match for poor Mr and Mrs Daubeney. He turned them out through the window without effort, and into the marquee, where for some time they waited in solitude under the steaming canvas; no chairs were provided. Having come south from Durham for the occasion they would have wished to rejoin those many Tilneys to whom they had so expectantly nodded in church.

Janet Studdart had been told by her family to 'cope' with Lady Elfrida, but soon gave this up. She paced here and there, a heavy-lidded and rather sombre Diana, supervising the Wolf Cubs. She looked darkly in at the Daubeneys in the marquee and remarked what a good thing it was that the afternoon had cleared up.

'Some more will be coming out,' she added, 'but just now there seems to be a stoppage. Do you know Cheltenham?'

The Daubeneys did not.

'It's stuffy,' said Janet. 'Even we notice that, although we live here. And of course weddings are tiring. It's a pity,' she added, looking dispassionately round the marquee, 'you can't sit down.'

Mrs Daubeney said faintly: 'We like standing.' This tall, rather fierce girl did not make a pleasurable impression on the Daubeneys, though obviously seeking to be kind. She now blew a blast on a whistle, piercingly and abruptly, issued an order to a Wolf Cub and disappeared. Mrs Daubeney supposed that daughters of retired colonels living outside Cheltenham often did this. How fortunate Laurel was to have married Edward; they would live in London and visit in Scotland and the North.

It had delighted the Studdarts to assemble at Laurel's wedding many old friends whose persistence had become a reproach and cousins receding in distance almost to vanishing-point. The Cliffords were here, whose greeting arrived each third week of December in time to be returned before Christmas; the Blakes so immersed in their Hampstead interests; the Bowleses always ready to put up the girls in Bayswater, to whom the girls never would go; the Thirdmans who had lived ten years in Switzerland and knew nobody. Alex and Willa Thirdman remained in the drawing-room doorway, turning this way and that their charming, anxious faces. They launched and abandoned smiles. They murmured: 'Surely that is Eliza Strang – over there by the cabinet – very much stouter. I don't think she sees us . . . And surely – no – yes – no – that is Lambert Cane?' But it seldom was. Lambert Cane, for instance, had died some years ago, with every formality. The Thirdmans were shockingly out of it. They had brought their girl, Theodora, for whom at each introduction they joyously turned. But she was never beside them. Theodora had, at the very first, said to her parents, 'I wish you would not *huddle*,' and angrily left them. Hearing a tinkle of spoons in the marquee and anxious for ices she had gained the buffet without being forced to acknowledge the bridal pair by the simple expedient of pushing her way through the hall door and walking round outside the house.

The bride's two attendants, little girls grilled to the waist, with pink knickers, had escaped from old gentlemen on to the spongy lawn. Here they were playing clock golf till the cake should be cut.

'Cheat!' shrieked Prue.

'Are you allowed almond-paste?' Dilly countered.

'Oo, I'm sick of old almond-paste!' Prue, swinging her putter, jumped as hard as she could to make dents in the green. 'I was bridesmaid once with a little boy that cried in the church. Were you ever?'

Mortified, Dilly putted in silence.

'I got a pearl pendant that time, and another time I got corals. What did you get ever?'

'Oh, you cheat you! You kicked your ball!'

'Oh, well, I'm not playing really; I call this a silly old game.'

Their four little pink satin shoes were green-stained. There would be trouble, Theodora noted with pleasure. She was fifteen and, except for the bridesmaids, the youngest present. Every allowance made for her unfortunate age, her appearance was not engaging. She was spectacled, large-boned and awkwardly anxious to make an impression. Her mother, with infinite solicitude, had chosen her for the occasion a large stiff blue hat. All the grown-up girls present wore droopy hats that cast a transparent shadow across their faces. She determined to persecute Mrs Thirdman for this on the way home. Pulling out her hair-ribbon under her hat, she entered the marquee, where she had some slight diffidence about approaching the buffet.

Mrs Daubeney engaged her attention by wearing a toque of violets like Queen Alexandra's, also a pearl collar. 'Let me get you an ice,' Theodora said boldly.

'Oh . . . I don't think they've quite begun.'

'I daresay I'll manage.'

Mrs Daubeney would have preferred tea. But certainly Edward had married into a tradition of capable girls, though she had heard he was highly-strung . . . With Mrs Daubeney, over two reluctantly granted ices, Theodora was enjoying what she was resigned to believe her unique success of the afternoon when Lady Elfrida joined them. Theodora looked strikingly at Edward's striking mother, but was ignored.

'Dear Edith,' exclaimed Lady Elfrida, 'I thought I should never find you – Ices? Oh how dreadful! – I hope your feet are not wet; mine are soaking; I think I shall die. Edward never was fortunate in his weather.'

'I don't think he has done so badly, Elfrida.'

'Oh, don't you? – I do want you to see Janet!'

'Janet?'

'You remember I told you –'

Mrs Daubeney lowered her voice, the tent was beginning to fill up. 'But Laurel is very pretty.'

'Oh yes, yes. Edward had to make up his own mind. She's lovely, isn't she? At his age –' Lady Elfrida's glittering look ran round the confused Mrs Daubeney like lightning. She looked derisive, and having already said far too much had the air of holding with ironic impatience more in reserve. She laughed. 'Janet's so *capable* – she's left two of those little Cubs in Edward's dressing-room to see no one puts rice in the suitcases. But at his age –'

From which Theodora, intently listening, inferred that Janet loved Edward, that his mother preferred Janet; that for Janet this was a day of chagrin, possibly of despair. Despair (wrapped up in curtain, biting the curtain) Theodora could understand, but not yet love. She felt an attraction to Janet and longed to find her. She could not help looking significantly at Lady Elfrida.

'I expect she has interests,' said Mrs Daubeney, remembering the whistle. Girls could not all expect to marry.

'Oh, but I don't believe in interests, do you?' said Lady Elfrida. At this point Theodora, opening her mouth to speak, saw Mrs Daubeney being removed by a skilful touch on the elbow. 'What a terrible girl,' said Lady Elfrida, who made no allowance for age, as they retreated. 'Who on earth –?'

'I have no idea,' said Mrs Daubeney.

Theodora remained looking gloomily down at the crushed grass. 'We shall meet again,' she assured herself. 'She will be anxious to know me.' On this occasion, Theodora had certainly not arrived. She had to confess inexperience; her personality was still too much for her, like a punt-pole. Surrendering to an advance from the kind Bowleses – was this her first English wedding? – she recurrently thought of Janet. Mrs Bowles would be delighted to put Theodora up when she came to London.

'We live in London, thank you,' said Theodora. 'We have a flat.'

Someone very tall appeared in the French window. 'What a marvellous young man!' said Theodora loudly.

'Ssh,' whispered Mrs Bowles, 'that is the bridegroom. They will be coming out to cut the cake.' Theodora looked at Edward and, for one delusive moment, loved him.

The wedding went off delightfully. No one, even the bride, remained for more than a second clearly in view; there was some rather poignant gaiety, some confusion. The Cheltenham caterer justified his reputation. The little bridesmaids dived shrieking in and out of the marquee, tripping over the tent-cords. Laurel, very much elated, not nervous, cut a slice from the cake and traced another; Edward said surely that was enough; Janet took her place. Lewis Gibson, the best man, feared Janet might find this too much. Healths were proposed. The bride and bridegroom, the best man and the bridesmaids were photographed. The sun descended, the wet garden was staged in light; guests ventured out on duck-boards to see the tulips. The sun, still descending, came in at the side of the marquee, painting the company. Laughter became expressed in glittering teeth, congeniality in a flashing eyeglass. A white kid glove rolled back from a wrist, the half-ruined cake went golden; the faces flame-coloured – Lady Elfrida's was for a moment ravaged: she had this less than moment for consternation, her own life was ruined, ruined – The moment went unseen. The little girls were given champagne, champagne was taken away from the little girls. One of the Studdarts' friends said to one of the Tilneys' friends, she hoped they might meet again: this, alas, was impossible, for the Tilneys' friend was going abroad. One of the Tilneys' friends asked one of the Studdarts' friends to lunch, to help her organize something. Someone felt faint in the marquee. Someone showed some disposition to weep. Word came that the bride and bridegroom were going away.

Mrs. Studdart had the last word. Leaning into the car she added: 'And Laurel you *must* remember to write about the candlesticks. And there are those two lamps and the coffee-tray. I have put a list in your dressing-case.'

'Oh yes, Mother, yes.'

'I daresay Edward has letters too.'

Edward, who did not think it delicate on Mrs Studdart's part to allot their immediate future, nodded with some reserve and the Daimler presently moved off.

The photographer's proofs arrived some days afterwards. The wedding group was not an entire success. The best man's spectacles glared, belying his natural mildness; the young bridesmaids had 'over-posed' and showed too much knee. All the same, copies were very much in demand. The young couple, mounted, framed, soon took up life in Corunna Lodge. Their height, their grace had been transferred to the plate; their youth with its suggestion of the heroic perhaps exaggerated a little. When one called at Corunna Lodge, if one said nothing, Mrs Studdart could never resist moving the photograph forward. Even the stranger, the casual visitor, could infer much of Laurel: her fairness, her charm, her irregular prettiness, the tilt of the long eyes, the turn of the head, the rueful gay smile that would be for less than a moment. She appeared delicious. And Edward – the forehead, the eyes set not very deep in their deep sockets, the short jutting nose with wide delicate nostrils, the line of the jaw square, too fine to be massive: formality, a surviving childish gravity and elegance, perversity, incuriosity, impassibility, communicativeness. His smile, Mrs Studdart explained, did not appear. But, as Janet added, his smile was not expressive.

2

For the Studdarts, the summer of 192– was to prove eventful. They came to be notable among the families of Cheltenham; it was supposed by the neighbourhood that early marriages really must run in families, and that since Mrs Studdart herself had married just out of her 'teens, her girls had been born to this happy tradition. Six weeks after the wedding of Laurel, Janet announced her engagement to Rodney Meggatt. She had not, these difficult days, been expected to marry; she had little charm, many interests, appeared even forbidding. Letters began to come in again steadily; Mrs Studdart had hardly a pause in her correspondence. By this time she had learned to reply by formula, and for hours set aside daily she verbally smiled and puckered. Where, indeed, would she be without her girls? But as a mother one lived for these deprivations. Once, unaccountably, in the course of a morning she crossed the room to kiss Janet who, at her typewriter, wound up her dealings with several local societies before resigning the secretaryships.

'I suppose it's never possible to be absolutely sincere,' said Mrs Studdart in confidence – as though the girl were married already. But Janet, barely pausing over the keys, looked blankly up with her very dark eyes. If in her twenty years she had formed opinions, she never expressed them. No one knew what she thought. She had now, of course, her happiness, but it had been difficult – Cheltenham did not know.

A fortnight after her sister's wedding, when everything was cleared up and the house quiet, she had gone to visit in —shire (the invitation arising out of the wedding), taking three new dresses given her by her father as a reward for having been so busy and capable, as a consolation because she was not the bride. Once or twice at least, by day and by night, she would be, in her dark way, certain to look beautiful. She wrote to her mother three times: first, that weather in —shire was uncertain; rain interrupting a tennis party at Batts Monachorum she had played billiards throughout the afternoon with a Rodney Meggatt, nephew of Considine Meggatt at Batts Abbey (the explorer and big-game hunter). Then, that she and Margaret were sitting up all night with Margaret's borzoi which had distemper; Margaret wanted her to stay on. Finally, that the borzoi was better; that Rodney Meggatt, who had ridden over several times to inquire for the borzoi, wanted to marry her and that she, for her part, would like to marry him. She came home two days afterwards to discuss the project; Rodney, by invitation, followed. It seemed hardly credible. Rodney was fair, lean but solid; his manner quiet but with, at this time, an undertone of excitement. He was very much liked in —shire; Colonel and Mrs Studdart immediately understood why. Naturally, they were pleased. Janet's creamy-pale face had the repose of serenity; her slow smile sent up her cheeks in lovely curves under downcast eyelids; her rare dark look remained as ever intent, searching, with nothing of a child's in it but an oblique directness that paused and turned away. It had passed for sullenness, this habit of looking down. But her reserve of expression could now hide nothing but happiness.

But presently they had been appalled; there appeared a substantial difficulty, a cruel obstacle. Before the appearance of Edward last autumn, from over the Cotswolds, and his rather dazzling courtship of the entire family which had not for some months particularized in the direction of Laurel, the Studdarts had known nothing of the Tilneys. Their worlds were apart. Edward's mother's distressing past was no more than a fact to them; into its details – out of delicacy, awkwardness, solicitude for Edward – they had not even now cared to enter. Edward, it had been easy to satisfy themselves, was himself irreproachable. Now it was Laurel who wrote from Dalmatia, desperate with apprehension. Meggatt? *Meggatt?* Was it possible that they did not know? Rodney's uncle Considine had been Lady Elfrida's corespondent.

Letters on this affair of extreme delicacy shot to and fro between the distracted Studdarts in Cheltenham and the distracted young Tilneys honeymooning in Dalmatia. Rodney had to be asked to be most considerate and withdraw for a short time, perhaps for a

short time only. There was nothing for Janet to say; she wrote to
nobody. Hearts bled for her; her happiness had been interdicted.
Mercifully, the Girl Guides kept her busy during this difficult
period: a rally was being organized. Meanwhile, which to
approach first: Considine (appreciative of Janet, affably disposed
towards the Studdarts, unaware – apparently – of the Tilney
connection) or Lady Elfrida, unconcernedly elsewhere, they
thought Venice? The Studdarts had not liked to suggest that
Edward should write to his mother; it was Laurel who urged this.

In indirect reply to Edward's communication, Lady Elfrida
wrote promptly to Cheltenham. She did not consider the situation
awkward at all. Not nowadays when everybody was different,
everyone else dead. She thanked the Studdarts but was unable to
understand them. Why sacrifice Janet? If Rodney were like his
uncle she could wish Janet no one better – and how she loved her!
Considine surely, surely did not object? She would write at once
to him. Surely nothing so far-fetched should stand in the way of
Janet's happiness? Especially since Edward – here, with unusual
thoroughness, she had scratched half a sentence out. Concluding,
she wished they were all in Venice, which was delightful.

To Edward she wrote to the same effect, tartly. She had reasons
for her annoyance; a rapid and superficial reader, she had found
his letter, all qualifications qualified, almost unintelligible. She
hoped (but apparently without confidence) that he and Laurel
were having a nice time in Dalmatia.

Gravely, shut up in the morning-room, Colonel and Mrs Studdart re-read and talked over Lady Elfrida's letter. Dimly, they
appreciated their own difficulty, which was that they were neither
quite worldly nor quite unworldly enough to be either high-
handed or simple about the matter. They did not know if they
were reasonable, trying to be good, or good, trying to be reasonable. They were shocked by Lady Elfrida's attitude and did not
know whether to condemn her as a lady or as a woman. Colonel
Studdart, who did not like a woman to be dispassionate, suspected
she was not wholly either. Yet here they were, bound to gratitude,
for she tossed their daughter happiness, an establishment, with a
negligent hand.

They pictured the Abbey with cedars, cypresses; their daughter
walking cheerfully over the smooth lawns. Rodney was Considine's heir; his uncle had not married. Colonel Studdart thought

17

of the shooting, but put this behind him. His wife, however, was not ashamed to enter the garden and pace in minute examination down border after border. They had from the first liked Rodney better than Edward, and as they both loved Janet a little less than Laurel they felt Rodney was owed to her. The growing-up together of Meggatt and Tilney children might well heal the ugliness of that adultery, cheerfully re-linking the two names.

Colonel and Mrs Studdart agreed upon nothing, decided nothing, but suddenly, solemnly kissed. She went out to look for Janet. There was nothing particular to say: Janet, in uniform, was half on to her bicycle, in a hurry; this was the day of the rally. Her mother gave her Lady Elfrida's letter, at which she had less than a moment to glance. Then Janet skimmed off round the circular grass plot and out of the gate with the stucco lions. There would be always her interests.

Rodney, recalled by telegram, was there for dinner when Janet returned from the rally very tired. Later, he and she walked down the garden, hardly able to distinguish each other in the mild starlight. The air was heavy with a chestnut's foliage and thousand unlit candles. Past the chestnut, by the poplars, she wept on his shoulder; one would have said with despair. He barely bent his head, they were both very tall. They did not speak; till now he had hardly touched or kissed her. Though she did not love him she began to understand desire. He comforted her a little. A week later, their engagement was announced. Then Cheltenham knew that both the Studdart girls would in a summer, a summer when men were so few, have married with ease and simplicity, and married well. Janet's wedding, however, would not take place till the autumn.

So Mrs Studdart was at her writing-table, morning after morning, regretting there was no absolute insincerity. She did not again kiss Janet so unaccountably. And Janet, leaving the affairs of the local organizations in perfect order, handed over to other secretaries – who hoped their own terms of office might be as brief, for as happy reasons. She received some engraved silver presents in recognition; these were a delight to her parents.

Lady Elfrida, in a subsequent letter to Janet, spoke of a purely personal disappointment. She had hoped she and Janet might have been much together. She was by now back from Venice and, writing from Trevor Square, painted herself as solitary. Would

18

Janet come to her at the end of June? Together, they might project the trousseau. (She had delayed some four days in Paris, where autumn – in the Trade's desperate prematurity – already foreshadowed the Place Vendôme, and the oracles, though still mute, had significantly gestured.) One understood that Rodney would be, at this time, also in London. (In the post-war, prolonged indecision his bent had not yet declared itself; meanwhile he had obtained through the influence of his uncle an interesting secretaryship.)

Mrs Studdart declared herself resigned to the visit; even, after a day's consideration, favourable. Janet must take a bold line. It seemed best for Janet to crash forthwith, before marriage, through this thicket of implications. Two or three difficult *tête-à-têtes*, some triangular awkwardness; much not said when the young Tilneys returned to town (and at the thought of Edward's return to town Mrs Studdart did shut her eyes defensively) and her Janet would have established and fortified her extraordinary position. Only as to the trousseau, Mrs Studdart advised Janet not to let Lady Elfrida influence her unduly. She did *know*, naturally, but was perhaps extreme. But it would be nice for Janet to see some models and take some patterns. Janet agreed. She had, however, secretly set her heart on a gold wedding-dress, of which she meant to speak for the first time to Lady Elfrida. She was to be an October bride: one could forecast chrysanthemums, a certain quality in the sunshine. Janet (though she did not clearly formulate this or any idea) personified Weather as someone feminine, tractable while perverse, agreeably subject to the dominance of some wills, upon whom Rodney could not fail to exercise a compulsion. Nothing should impair his magnificence as a bridegroom. Edward's appeal had notably failed with the demigoddess. She thought, perhaps to love Edward one must be half a man.

June afternoon, in Knightsbridge, polished the house-fronts; a crystal twirled in a window; the young town trees, the curtains were mildly sensitive to a breeze. Life in the streets and squares ran transparent and ran without a ripple. A foot on a step, a door opening, a taxi stopping engaged the street; the balconies shared a calm social expectancy. Janet found Lady Elfrida's long little drawing-room green, cool, receptive – the sun was off it – her hostess quite haggard with the anticipation of pleasure. Lady Elfrida, whose journeys were seldom less than transcontinental, ignored the transition from Cheltenham; she did not ask if Janet were tired but, displacing a Siamese cat from the sofa beside her, drew Janet down at once to a level of intimate talk among the cushions.

'You're looking wonderful: how this suits you. We will have tea, but listen – Edward and Laurel are back. (But you know, I expect?) They are just the same, not surprised at all. They will talk of nothing but what they saw in Dalmatia.'

'But Laurel has travelled so little.'

'But it cannot be so different.'

Janet, taking her gloves off slowly because of her shyness, said, 'Laurel sees everything new.' Lady Elfrida, who did not care to understand Laurel, went on rapidly:

'And in their house they are making every mistake. I thought perhaps *you* – I can't, you see. They are like sparrows tugging little pieces of things about; little patterns, you know, of the wrong brocades. Of course they don't know where to go for their things; it is difficult for them. I think they rely on you. I lunched there today and didn't know what to say. It is all like a little girl's first room of her own, without even the daisies. You or I – Janet, how old are you?'

Janet said: 'Twenty.' In view of her capability and composure the statement was hardly ever received without surprise. It went without saying, she looked older than Laurel. Early, while her hair was still down her back, she had accepted maturity; as though someone touching her on the shoulder had told her to come away from a party that had hardly begun.

'Twenty? That was when I married. Now show me your ring – Oh yes, I like Rodney; I knew he was wise. He does know your hands, doesn't he? When shall we meet?'

'Rodney? I don't think tonight . . .'

'No, I thought of the Opera. Oh, you are tired: how foolish I am.' And Lady Elfrida, in her solicitude, poured out tea more quietly. Perhaps she thought: 'Janet gets tired easily.' The Siamese, reappearing like a malign sun over the cushions, looked at his mistress with penetration, without sympathy. She did not evoke sympathy; she had few friends, for she appeared to lack reticence and talked extravagantly, exaggerating her idea of her-

self. Loved, she exasperated the affection; the indignation of
Edward's gentle father had been cumulative and upon discovery
of her deception he had divorced her punitively. Her abandonment of Considine, his abandonment of her, remained inexplic-
able. Tall mirrors prolonged her little drawing-room in false
perspectives; in her life as in her drawing-room an acquaintance,
losing the sense of direction, hardly knew which way to proceed.
She put down a saucer of milk for the Siamese, which dropped to
it like a plummet from the sofa-back, startling Janet.

3

Edward said to Laurel, very early in the morning after Janet's
arrival at Trevor Square: 'I suppose we ought to have a family
lunch?'
'Four?' said Laurel. What resolution he had!
'Rodney.'
'Not five – your mother?'
'Four,' repeated Edward, turning over in bed.
'Oh ...?' said Laurel. The protest was quite perfunctory;
Laurel did feel very much relieved. For after lunch yesterday,
when Lady Elfrida had gone, she had asked herself, 'What is the
good?' realized some lives could never approach and longed to
telephone to Cheltenham. She returned all the patterns Lady
Elfrida deprecated to the wrong shops and was in tears when
Edward came home because they would never have any curtains
now.
Edward always woke full of determination. Now, blinking up
from the pillow at a curtainless brilliant window, he resumed:
'Not, of course, today.' They lay side by side on their two low
beds as on tombs and were each aware in the other, falling asleep,
of the same carven air of finality. Now, shading their eyes,
they turned to discover each other again in the light of the new
day.
'Perhaps not today.' Determining in her heart to be first with
Janet alone, she put out a hand; their fingers groped for each
other over the chasm between the beds. A small thrill animated
the tombs. Tomorrow, then, they should all four lunch together

at the Ionides. Laurel got up to go to her bath and Edward fell asleep again.

As soon as Edward had left the house for Whitehall Laurel ran to the telephone. Janet was barely awake – Lady Elfrida with what seemed to Laurel an infinite lack of consideration had taken her to the Opera. The two laughed with pleasure at the sound of each other's voices; for some minutes no plans were formulated. Each, in effect, promised: 'I'll tell you my secret,' and for those minutes it was as though Lady Elfrida had never sinned. Then there was a slight break, Janet's voice changed and on Lady Elfrida's behalf she wished Laurel good morning. She promised to come round to Royal Avenue at half-past eleven.

Lady Elfrida, who had and desired no sister, was prepared to countenance the relationship only quite superficially. Laurel could guess at her disappointment. There would have certainly been a morning, a today projected for Trevor Square that should admit only Rodney. But her hostess would find Laurel's sister adamant. Laurel attempted pity. 'Elfrida's like me,' she thought, 'she sets her heart on things.'

At half-past eleven Laurel, posted up at her drawing-room window, watched a tall couple walk down Royal Avenue. She felt some admiration: Rodney. Opposite her door they parted: one had a good view of him. Janet did not look back at her lover; a moment later the bell rang. The sisters met on the staircase. In her dark clothes, with her new assurance, a rose pinned into her coat, Janet appeared more than ever distinguished.

Surprised by their emotion (for they had hardly missed one another) they drew apart a little but smilingly paced the room. 'Look . . .' Laurel exclaimed. 'We have no taste!' She pointed out to her sister a chair, a rug, a green lacquer cabinet where she knew they had erred, sat down in the brightest armchair to cover most of it, and went on to tell Janet how she was a true bride, terrified of the servants – she had planned years ago servants of hers should wear mob caps and cherry-pink in the mornings, but Simpkins and Sylvia (what a name for a cook!) were not to be imposed upon – and changing her new dresses, for very exhilaration, three times a day. She liked London better even than she had expected, and carried (though Edward must never suspect this) a map of it in her handbag, also a guide to the buses. It was still odd to think of a London day not in terms of shopping, and of districts out of relation to Paddington station. Mrs Bowles had already rung up to ask if there was anything she could do. And the girl Theodora Thirdman had rung up, no one could think why. Laurel confessed: 'At the wedding, I asked her to stay. She made me so nervous, I could not think what else to say. But as they are living in London I don't think she can want to, do you?'

Janet thought not. It occurred to Laurel, pausing in her talk, how odd it was that Janet should not have mentioned Rodney, though he had come to the very door. With a shade of resentment, Laurel began to talk again, rapidly: Janet seemed quite a stranger.

Janet looked round her, recognizing the wedding presents. She knew them all too well, better than Laurel; she had unpacked, arranged and re-packed them, wondering how they could all come together to make a home. She was relieved that the room did not look like an exhibition; she said so to Laurel. Sun streamed in generously; from chairs and cushions colour must already be making a ghostly departure.

'Oh, Janet –'

Janet, who seldom smoked, took a cigarette from the shagreen box and lit it seriously.

'– we *didn't* spoil your engagement? You didn't spoil our honeymoon!'

'It worried mother and father. But I knew Rodney and I would marry.'

'Does Rodney not mind at all?'

'You see, he is accustomed to Considine. I suppose Considine is impossible. There have been several – I mean there are so many people Rodney could not marry if he let himself look at things that way.'

Janet did seem cynical. And this was, in a desperate way, funny. Half Laurel's smiles were against her judgement; one came now, irresponsible as a butterfly. 'What a good thing he's so much in Africa! What's he like – Considine?'

'I don't know: I do like him.'

'Janet, you *are* very –? I mean, aren't you fearfully –? You know I can't ask.'

Looking down, at the question about her happiness, Janet landed her ash in the little tray with lotuses. 'I've never felt like this before,' she said accurately. Laurel's moment towards her disappeared like a thought, forbidden. Disappointed, she could

not help saying: 'I don't think Edward's going to mind very much
any more.'

'Oh,' said Janet, without irony.

'But if you had any idea – if you could understand, Janet, how
fearful it's always been for him about Elfrida. I don't expect I
really quite understand, yet. You and I've never had to cope with
these things.'

Janet's eyelids remained inexpressive. Laurel went on, with her
new little wise air of having been schooled in humanity: 'You
know, you do sometimes talk, Janet, as though everything in the
world that had happened had happened to yourself and you were
resigned to it, so it didn't matter. But after all, you aren't Edward.
Nobody else is. When he was five they all came . . .'

'. . . Who all came?'

'His Tilney aunts. They came without any explanation and
took him away from his home in a cab, so indignantly. He says
that's what he remembers so fearfully; nobody would explain.
A dreadful house in Buckinghamshire appeared from somewhere
and bits of the London furniture kept turning up in it; like wreckage coming down on a flood, he thought.'

'Really, Edward can't have thought of that when he was *five*.
I do think, Laurel, it's time you gave him something else to think
about. If he had even been nine or ten . . .'

'Well, he was five,' said Laurel, annoyed. 'When he was six
he asked if his mother was dead and they said, "Practically." You
can imagine what he felt about that; he had just seen a skeleton.'

'Were his aunts unmarried?'

'Of course. Meanwhile, *she* was living alone, so reproachfully,
over in Paris. Edward says he would not like to say that Considine
had deserted her, but it did seem to everyone extraordinary that
they did not marry. It really did seem as though she had thought
out what she ought not to do, what to avoid, what would hurt
people most, and done it all. Then people began to say how unfortunate she was, then how charming, then just when Edward
was at the most sensitive age she came back to England for the
war and seemed to be everywhere. Edward had grown up always
meaning to comfort her and to re-establish her, and when they did
meet he was absolutely nonplussed. Then she worked in a hospital
in the south of France, and when he had that last year of the war
in France, when he was nineteen, he spent his leaves with her.

When the war was over and he went to Oxford she took the Trevor Square house. She seemed absolutely contented and talked about Considine as though he were Edward's uncle, till he had to make her see that he couldn't bear it. Even then Considine kept turning up with lions and things in the *Tatler* and the *Illustrated London News*.'

'He is very distinguished.'

'Oh I know, I know; he might so well have been the hero of Edward's youth.'

'But he can't have made Edward a permanent invalid.'

But Janet was not yet a wife, how could she understand? Her husband had told Laurel all about this in the dark, with his head close to hers and his arms round her. Had he spoken of this before? He said, till now he had not ever let himself think or feel. Once she comforted him so much that he wept. They had designed, wordlessly, that he must re-live his childhood.

Laurel, spreading out her fingers on the arm of the chair, looked so much oppressed and in face of Janet's un-sympathy so lonely, that Janet moved over to be beside her. 'Darling, I'm sorry. But we must all live *somehow*. I suppose things are different for me; I don't feel much, I suppose. I've always had to do something, or arrange for something, or answer a letter. I don't even know what people are like – look how I couldn't tell you about Considine! I suppose Lady Elfrida is outrageous, but that just seems to be like her living in Trevor Square or never listening or being unpunctual or having dark-red hair.'

'Dyed,' flickered Laurel.

'And yet she is so imposing. This afternoon she is going to take me to some of those terrifying upstairs shops that Mother can't get out of. Really, Laurel, I think it must be a good thing for people to harden.'

'If people can,' said Laurel. '– Tell me about Rodney.'

'He is coming to dinner tonight.'

'But I must know *about* him!'

'He came here to the door with me. I thought perhaps you would see him.'

'I did,' Laurel admitted.

'Do you see what I mean?'

'About marrying him? Of course. But oh, Janet, do try and be less extraordinary! Perhaps when you're married . . .'

'Perhaps,' Janet said gravely. 'But I never shall be able to think of anything to say that is what I mean – Laurel, when can we all meet?' Laurel, with some forebodings which increased as she spoke, unfolded Edward's plan for tomorrow. Janet was touched. She was certain Rodney would be free. He must be free. Laurel said she was certain Edward would like Rodney. They did not again speak of Edward, or Rodney either. There seemed no reason why either topic, during the years ahead in which they were to live with their husbands, should come up again.

Sylvia the cook looked round the door at the head of the basement stairs. With interest she heard the sisters come downstairs to look at the dining-room. They crossed the hall; she had a good view of them. Now Mrs Tilney was a pretty little thing and anxious to please, but had no 'style'. One could see she was not accustomed to London ways; for instance, she had tried to suggest that Sylvia and Simpson should dress like waitresses in a fancy teashop, and naturally they were not going to stand for that. She was for ever bringing pictures down to the kitchen to make it cheerful; Sylvia understood her to be a clergyman's daughter. But Miss Studdart had style; it would not surprise Sylvia if she were to marry an Honourable. A wife like that would have been the makings of Mr Tilney, to get him out of his fanciful ways, which Sylvia did not feel she would be able to stand for more than a month or so, what with this thing and that thing, not to speak of Simpson's goings on: a girl like that would run after a Chelsea pensioner: anything in trousers. However, the work was light and she and Simpson had given Mrs Tilney plainly to understand she must not have a dog, children or dinner-parties.

At this point, a latchkey turned in the lock and Sylvia nearly stepped backwards downstairs with indignation. For here was Mr Tilney, popping back again when he was not due home till six; when Mrs Tilney was about to be given a poached egg on a tray and to be grateful for that. 'Just a bone,' he would say. 'As though,' thought Sylvia, 'we were a mortuary.'

The ladies came out of the dining-room where, by the sound of it, Mrs Tilney had been repolishing the table (one for Simpson). Mr Tilney stood blindly, as though the hall were the coal-hole. Putting out a hand to the dining-room door he said: 'My darling?'

And Miss Studdart said in her decided low voice: 'Hullo ... Edward.'

4

Theodora had hoped great things of the wedding. She was disappointed: socially, nothing had materialized. By the time the
young Tilneys were back from their honeymoon, she was still at a
standstill.

Theodora had a very clear view of her family's situation; it was
important that the Thirdmans, after long exile, should establish
themselves in England. During the train journey to Cheltenham,
she had implored her parents to make full use of this opportunity.
That desperation might do its full work she had left them, on the
return from church, advantageously placed in an archway between the two rooms. Here, however, exposed and fatally passive
they had been collected by the Bowleses. While she herself, disqualified by the hat, too anxiously roving, had prepossessed no
one. Her failure was written for her in large characters; she satisfied nothing but her appetite and at last, pale from over-indulgence, marzipan and ices, had taken her parents away from the
festive house. Returning, third class, knee-to-knee with the
Bowleses, she glowered a general disparagement from under her
bright hat. Alex and Willa Thirdman could never be made to see
life was one's affair and, at that, desperate. At their most positive,
they put up a little mild fortitude. Because of this, perhaps, their
daughter had armed herself like a bandit, to hold up anything,
anyone, and wreak pillage upon the years.

Alex and Willa Thirdman were satisfied with their afternoon;
having been overlooked with such affability they could no longer
regret Switzerland. Wistful, they pressed their faces against the
glass while the train's speed squandered the precious regained
fields; by each flashing gable or garden they momentarily dwelt
and pondered. Keen inquiries from the Bowleses elicited some
recollections of Switzerland – Apart from anything else, Theodora
thought the Bowleses were certainly damned, for they talked in
trains – Dear Switzerland, cleaner than Italy, kinder than France;
Willa extolled the air, milk, honesty, education, arrangement of
scenery; there but never too close. Hundreds of English families,
dotted in châlets along the lake, had been happy in their trans-
lation. There had been pleasures: boating, botany, the dear

League of Nations. The Bowleses congratulated Theodora upon being able to speak three languages.

Theodora glowered. She replied that this was untrue; her spectacles magnifying a horror of that cold lake, of the bleak excellence of her Swiss education. They recollected she was fifteen, a difficult age.

During those weeks of Laurel's honeymoon, Theodora became more than ever difficult. The Gloucester Road flat was too small for her, her large feet thundered among the hired bric-à-brac. The telephone became at once her distraction and torture. She would not go out with her parents, but solitary in the flat remained for hours with the directory, hearing the steps, the traffic go east to pleasure. Then, having bolted the door, she rang up several prominent people and, skilfully passing secretary or butler, maintained with each a conversation of some seconds, under the pseudonym of Lady Hunter Jervois. She had a pleasant, mature voice: an asset. Passionately passing along the wire she became for those moments the very nerve of some unseen house. But it was bitterness. She exclaimed once to Willa: 'Mother, are we so absolutely *superfluous*?'

'It will be nicer, dearest, when you're at school. But we thought –' They had thought, a term off, a cultural London holiday. From six, the girl had suffered a rigorous education.

'But don't we want to *matter* in this place? Aren't we ever going to begin? Mother, you're like someone sitting for always on a suitcase in a railway station. Such a comfortable suitcase, such a magnificent station! *Eeooch!*' She emitted an indescribable sound.

'Theodora, you really ought not to bully me.'

'I'm simply telling you –'

'Oh hush, Theodora. Father and I are disappointed; we thought you would like London.'

'What good is London to me?'

'Father and I are so happy going about on buses looking at all the types.'

'I hate types! And why does Father always carry a mackintosh?'

'We thought the galleries –'

'Entertainments we go to always seem to be free,' said her daughter suspiciously. 'Don't you *see* no one goes to galleries who has anything else to do?'

'But the National Gallery is always crowded, Theodora.'

'That just *shows*,' exclaimed Theodora. 'Can't you see that's why life's so awful?'

It certainly did seem difficult to be fifteen. Willa could just recall – herself, she had practised the piano a good deal, said, 'Very well, Father,' when Father objected; her figure began, she braided her back hair; there had been red-haired Mary and dark Mr Torrence – perhaps she had even loved? Had one been *difficile*? Willa could hardly think so. She clearly remembered saying: 'I'd really much rather not, thank you,' 'Just as you like, really,' and 'Indeed, Mrs X, I have no idea.'

Theodora improvised but did not practise; she did not seem likely to have a figure at all, so perhaps the soul was delayed also. So Willa said quietly: 'I expect Art will come.'

'I have no idea what you mean,' replied Theodora. At this point Alex Thirdman, coming in with his mackintosh from the South Kensington Museum, told Theodora she must not bully her mother. She went to bed, though it was four in the afternoon. So most discussions ended. She must have lain kicking her heels against the wall, for they heard thump – thump – thump against the thin partition. Mr and Mrs Thirdman sighed. Two days later they made a mysterious expedition into Surrey.

Here they interviewed a head mistress of, it seemed to them, striking originality, who set great store by individual development and encouraged her girls to keep pets. She understood at once what they meant about Theodora. 'She has a great deal of character,' Willa said, 'we can't help feeling she is a little unusual. She is highly strung and – I don't know how to explain – sensitive: she cannot be driven.' The head mistress received this calmly. 'We think she might write,' Willa added. But Alex – they were in the conservatory with the guinea-pigs – drew his stick softly along the bars of the cages: the guinea-pigs telescoped into their own fat, bumping back into darkness. 'She has a brain,' he said, staring into the cages (the brain his son would have had). 'But unsteady, variable.' The head mistress, a tall aquiline charmingly-dressed woman, approached Willa a little to intimate: 'Adolescence.' She had rows of books round her study to this heading. Guinea-pigs, thought Alex, guinea-pigs? He had forgotten – had Theodora missed something? The sun leaned hotly through the conservatory walls, they all flushed. Did Theodora form

29

strong attachments? They hardly knew! Switzerland was so temperate.

Following Miss Byng from the conservatory to the blue-green drawing-room – where pieces of modern statuary had been put about since Miss Byng feared no influence – they arranged for Theodora to be altogether an exception, to come at half-term, almost immediately. Because London . . . Miss Byng understood. She held in her ringless, nerveless hands their absolute confidence. There could be nothing she did not know about adolescence. A child running past the window in a scarlet tunic made happiness concrete, the lawns stood solid in sunshine, a piano-study issuing from a floor above built up a diligent self-rewarding pattern over this shining silence of application and still trees.

They were fortified, on their return to their girl: at last they had life to offer. The flat, darker than they expected, enclosed an ennui they had forgotten: Theodora had more than ever her caged air. She countered any announcement with an announcement: Laurel Tilney was back, Theodora had rung her up. Ring up so new a bride? They were appalled; it was impossible to explain why. And Studdarts really did seem to be in the air to-night, for here was a letter from Cheltenham: Janet, engaged, was to visit London. The situation of this new pair of lovers, so difficult, so perilous (and this time Theodora really had to be told why) engaged the Thirdmans' attention throughout dinner. Over the cool soup, the warm Canadian salmon, silent between the calm parental faces, Theodora meditated, testing the links of this new relationship. Considine – something came alive, she could perfectly see him: disengaged, blasé, rucking a tiger-skin, backed by the major feline masks, almost visibly shredded – like a fine, up-growing thistle on a cobwebby morning – with feminine reputations. Next morning she rang him up. For Considine, nothing was unlikely; there was nothing to tell him that the re-appearance of Lady Hunter Jervois might not be delightful (they had met, she said, too fleetingly in Cairo). He was charmed by the voice. But alas – she rang off and hurried to join her mother outside the tube station. They were to shop for school. Throughout the morning Theodora, ironically passive, had her teeth looked at, her eyes tested, was measured, revolved before the dispassionate mirrors of less expensive shops. By teatime she had acquired the boots, the ties, the tasselled cap, the knee-length tunic, the blazer, the 'rational' bodices and the dancing-sandals without which it was impossible for her personality to develop at Mellyfield. She sucked a lip, looking elsewhere. She had accepted the prospect of school without interest. 'For nothing,' as she said to her mother, disparaging through a window of their arrested bus the portentous delay of Oxford Street, 'nothing could be worse than this.'

Willa, in the marabout boa, massaging over each thumb her carefully cleaned gloves, was so much relieved. 'And you could take a dog, Theo.'

'I don't want a dog bought specially to go to school with.'

'They all seemed to have pets.'

'How extraordinary. Perhaps I could take a serpent.'

'I think hardly –'

'Show me the prospectus again.'

A quiet, reserved prospectus. But Theodora, turning over the pages, said: 'Oh my god!' Several people turned round in the bus. Illustrations: the girls running, at hockey, lacrosse and tennis, the girls preparing to dive, preparing to eat; the bathrooms, empty; the bedrooms, empty; the chapel, full; the swimming pool and the library. 'Really, Mother, you're touching . . .'

The bus ground on. It trembled slowly past Evans', where bright-coloured handkerchiefs darted across the glass like humming-birds and a grand wheel of stockings turned ceaselessly. Three-and-eleven: Willa looked back to admire. And meanwhile, deliberating along the curb, three tall girls, all like Janet, were visible to Theodora successively. She took this for a portent.

The very morning of Theodora's departure, Janet herself appeared in the Gloucester Road flat. Exhortations from Cheltenham prompted this visit. So dear, so forlorn, the Thirdmans constantly darkened her mother's moral horizon. One ought to do something, somehow . . . But with both her girls given over to love, such a large correspondence, the Lodge crowded . . . But the Thirdmans must not lapse. Hence Janet this morning, with nothing to say; an amiable deputation.

His wife packing for his daughter, his daughter criticizing his wife, Alex Thirdman, reading nothing of interest, received the visitor with delight. (For a moment she had a glimpse of vacancy.) He congratulated the straightforward girl on her engagement, then brought out, by inspiration, Theodora's new racquet to show her. Did she think this the best kind of racquet for Theodora?

At Lausanne the girl had once just missed a junior championship. Janet made no pronouncement hastily, she stood looking down, weighing the racquet. Alex, melancholy, a shade self-derisive, awaited the verdict. Had he failed as a father? He knew he would know now for always. The flat doors all clicked in the summer wind.

But Willa came in with an exclamation, plucking strands of darning wool from her dress.

'Janet, this is delightful! Theodora is going away to school today!'

'Then I'm afraid I have come on a bad morning.'

'Oh, I don't mean that *at all*. That is not at all what I meant – Where are you staying?'

'With Lady Elfrida.'

What a question, thought Willa, to have asked, when it was all so difficult. When the Tilneys had taken that line – could Rodney visit there? One did not know what was being said, one saw nobody; one longed to know what anyone else would have thought. 'Let me see,' she said, 'she lives near Harrod's, doesn't she? That must be very nice.'

'Oh yes, it is,' said Janet, 'very.'

A silence hovered; Janet had forgotten her mother's messages to the Thirdmans and had not the wit to invent others. She wondered what the Thirdmans would like to hear. These last weeks she had noticed someone who was herself for the first time, she could see nothing nowadays but herself, a figure she watched with fatalism. It was as though she had become shortsighted, almost everything was a blur and her looks to any distance naturally lacked direction. So she could not think of any news from Cheltenham except that all the dogs but one were being given away, as she would not be there to exercise them. She could have added, the fine weather for Rodney's wedding had already set in ahead, or was rehearsing, giving the hills and trees round Corunna Lodge, on afternoons when he came to see her, an eager brightness.

'School?' she repeated kindly. 'I hope she will be happy.' And on Theodora's coming in to shake hands, this was modified to: 'I hope you will like it,' because the two were near enough in a generation for it to be impossible to speak of happiness to one another.

'Of course, I have been to school before,' said Theodora. She

had had time to stage her entrance; her hair was tied back with
a bow of new stiff black ribbon. Hearing Janet's voice she had
changed her tie and remained a moment or two to project an
'impression'. She now stood, square in her new coat and skirt, all
spectacles, challenging Janet's composure. 'I daresay I may like
it all right,' she continued. 'One might as well see. They seem to
have taken a good deal of trouble with chintz and radiators and
things, and apparently you don't have to work unless you like; it
is individual development. The girls look rather foolish, but I
suppose it is unfair to judge from a prospectus. Of course, a great
deal will depend on whether I like them.'

'And if they like you,' said Janet naïvely. Theodora looked
sharply at her; they sat down on the sofa. 'What are nature
rambles?' Theodora continued.

'Botany.'

'Oh goodness, *that*. When are you going to be married?'

'October.'

Theodora said with some satisfaction: 'I shall be quite accustomed to school by *then*.' A bride seemed to her very unexperi-
enced beside a girl in her second term. Willa wondered, meanwhile, whether one could wear the same hat for Janet's and
Laurel's weddings. Perhaps some slight alteration, a rose for a
wing. She did not think anybody had noticed her hat much. Only
Alex – so scrupulous, so ineffectual, watching the scene, apart
from his own sex through little denials of life at every juncture,
apart from this feminine interaction, the competitiveness they all
set up – Alex had eyes for his wife's cousin, who sitting so gracefully upright among the hard satin cushions appeared withdrawn,
never among them, a positive no-presence. He had a pang for
those calm lips and saluted a woman he would have feared to love.
He went over to shut the clicking door. For the chicken browning
in the gas oven for Theodora's last luncheon was beginning to
make itself known in the little drawing-room.

Theodora was aware of the chicken with pleasure; for the
moment, home life had its compensations. 'This is my last day,'
she said royally. 'Please will you stay to luncheon? I am having
everything that I ask for.'

But alas, Janet could not. She was lunching with Laurel,
Edward and Rodney at the Ionides. She must be off now.

'*And* Lady Elfrida?'

'No, not today.'

'Have Rodney and Edward met before?'

'Never,' said Janet.

Possibly Lady Elfrida was disappointed. Possibly, thought Theodora, she, excluded, wept. For herself, she could not have imagined such disappointment. 'I am being put out of the way,' she thought of Mellyfield angrily. 'I am like a dog going to the lethal chamber.' She went with Janet to the door of the lift.

'Write!' she shouted.

But Janet only called up 'Good-bye', disappearing.

Soon the chicken was eaten and Theodora, by her own specific wish unaccompanied, was in the train for Mellyfield.

5

Edward and Rodney arrived at the Ionides some minutes before either Laurel or Janet. Janet had miscalculated the distance from Gloucester Road and Laurel had changed her dress twice. Across the small vestibule Edward observed Rodney: with each a suspicion of the other's identity deepened. Rodney, so fair and square, had the advantage of looking impassable. Finally, it had to be Edward who spoke.

Rodney shook hands cordially. His calm look took in nothing of Edward; he seemed content to be put off with Edward's rather too easy good manners. Possibly he may have felt he already knew him well. Responsibility remained with Edward, who remarked: 'I've got a table.'

'Good.'

It was at all times difficult for Edward to conceal his natural fussiness. 'I ought,' he said, 'to have told Laurel one-fifteen for one-thirty. She's always late.'

'Janet is always punctual,' said Rodney tranquilly. 'I suppose something's delayed her. She went to look up some people in Kensington.'

'The Thirdmans.'

'I daresay,' agreed Rodney, as though it struck him that Edward was full of information.

They might have had a drink, but Edward knew Laurel would

never find the table. She would sit down distractedly at someone else's, and reproach Edward afterwards for the mistake. They had both thrown cigarettes away and now brought their cases out simultaneously; Edward had one of Rodney's, but Rodney preferred his own. He seemed likeable, a scrupulous, slow young man, without the disengagedness of Considine, that light-hearted, light-handed seducer who (Edward had come to believe) even shot lions negligently.

A taxi ground off and Laurel, beautifully flushed, appeared in the doorway in summer green. Not for nothing had she hesitated among her wardrobe. 'The traffic,' she said. 'You have no idea. And Sylvia kept me – oh!'

During the introduction she was, involuntarily, defensive, startled. But the nephew of the destructive uncle smiled, already possessive. Already the brother-in-law. Beyond this, she could get no grasp of him; could guess at nothing but that he was certainly pleased. Meggatt men, she thought, get what they wanted calmly, in the course of their day. They had got Batts Abbey and abbey-lands out of Henry VIII.

'It is delightful to meet,' she said, still with faint resentment, while Edward, in implied reproof of the future Mrs Meggatt, again glanced at the time. While Rodney still conveyed a serious amiability, Janet, getting out unhurried, paid off her taxi. Rodney's look narrowed; love became momentously present and the young Tilneys, obliterated, wanted to walk away. Recollecting their own passion they rallied and were benevolent. Janet greeted them all equably; she had had no idea she was so late.

Edward ordered an excellent lunch but was, as politely as possible, not hungry. Laurel, who was greedy, enjoyed herself. Though she had groaned to Edward in the black of last night, 'What on earth shall we all talk about?' (when he had replied, his face in her hair: 'You are lovely') she forgot herself – an objective in manners her mother had constantly put before her – in the determination to set them all at ease. Edward, watching her critically, thought it must take Cheltenham to produce such a deep sense of social responsibility. Smiling a little wildly under her green hat she sipped Chablis, allowed no pause and dug little pink scoops out of her canteloupe. She presently caught Edward's eye and put down her spoon. There they all were, animated. But oh dear, had she overdone it?

'There is Owen Nares,' said Rodney, directing her attention politely. And presently there was the arrival of the sole.

One could not say Edward was less amiable than Laurel, but he remained guarded. Janet once or twice looked speculatively at him. Was he going to be difficult? Surely he could not wish one to take up 'a position'? In this restaurant full of determinedly 'interesting' people, Edward provoked other glances of speculation: his youthful haggardness, that smile with the rather delightful broadening of the nostrils, so misleadingly sardonic . . . His eyebrows, arching and contracting, became fretful under any too prolonged regard. 'No, no, you're quite mistaken; I am a civil servant. My sensibility is my own affair. Look elsewhere, please.'

So Janet, deliberately not looking, thought with her cold dispassionate passion, 'I could hold you, yes, and make you run about, in the palm of my hand.'

At a point half-way through luncheon it became evident to the watchful sisters that Edward and Rodney liked each other. The young women almost exchanged glances. The atmosphere became less conscious and the conversation was allowed to relax. Edward and Rodney discovered so many acquaintances in common, it appeared to Edward extraordinary that they had not met before. 'Odd,' he repeated. Rodney nodded; you could not tell what he thought. He had quite liked Edward from the moment they met, and perhaps more than ever wondered what all this fuss had been about. Once or twice Edward, a trifle put off by his manner, again recollected his mother weeping in Paris. For it must be remembered that Rodney had in no way repudiated, or authorized Janet to repudiate, his uncle Considine.

'Janet tells me your house is charming,' Rodney said to Laurel. 'Nobody else thinks so,' she replied with feeling. And after lunch, when Edward had got to get back to Whitehall, it was arranged that Rodney should drive the sisters back to Royal Avenue.

Laurel watched Edward hurry away with regret; she longed to know what he thought, how the lunch had gone off, whether Rodney had seemed at all embarrassed; if the green hat had really looked nice. With Janet so much was impossible . . . But while Rodney delayed a moment with Edward, the sisters getting into the taxi hastily kissed, as though in explanation.

6

Lady Elfrida was glad to infer the lunch had gone off well.

Rodney came round to Trevor Square about six, to find Janet still out. (For Laurel's curtains the afternoon was to be decisive; hurrying round London the sisters had brought back many more patterns to Royal Avenue and still sat among them.) Lady Elfrida had just come in from nowhere particular. Her gloves in her hand, she stood regretting the bright streets, at war with silence. The drawing-room, a plane tree in the court at the back flickering in its well of bright shadow, seemed in spite of her presence remarkably empty. She was delighted to see Rodney, her world resumed its tempo. They had met, of course, last night.

'So you all had lunch. How was Edward?'

'Very well,' said Rodney, with his pleasant formality. Very large, he took up his position before her fireplace: she, a man's woman, looked up in appreciation. For his part, he had been prepared for her as unfortunate: he had had no idea she would be amusing. Though, knowing his Considine, Rodney might well have guessed.

'Well, that was that,' she said. 'Edward, you know, finds things so difficult.'

'Oh?' said Rodney. He recollected having heard that she was impossible. She was certainly feminine, and because she chose to appear rather charmingly muddled and inconsequent he set her down as astute, more astute than she was. Brought up on Considine's cheerful ruthless generalizations as to the Sex, Rodney reacted towards a careful slowness of judgement on any woman. The Sex did not interest him; till now they had, as persons, appeared alarmingly like one another in only one particular: an aptness to set stages out on to which one stepped unawares and where it was impossible to behave without consciousness. Janet had pleased him by a rather masculine unawareness of 'situation'.

Though he stepped carefully, Rodney could not help enjoying Lady Elfrida's company. More alive than a young girl, pulling down the cushions round her, she communicated a delight in her own indiscretion. Rodney could see how it was that one came to gossip.

'And Laurel?'

'How very attractive and pretty!'

'Oh, don't underrate her; she has a character of her own.'

'She looks very happy.'

'She loves being married.'

'She certainly isn't at all like Janet.'

'Beautifully unlike,' she said with emphasis. The Siamese cat slid past Rodney's legs as he slowly looked at her in surprise.

'I mean otherwise Janet ought not to have a sister at all. I always feel, with women, the mould should be broken, not used again and again.'

'Oh?' said Rodney.

'Do tell me, where are you going to live?'

He hesitated, but this was bound to come up. 'Considine wants us to live at Batts. His idea is to make the place over to me. He's abroad so much and hates to think of the place shut up.'

'I'd no idea he cared so much for it –'

'Well, perhaps he thinks I hate to think of it shut up,' said Rodney accurately. 'He promises he would make his home with us when he's in England. He seems determined Janet –'

'But Janet told me you were going to live in London.'

'I think she feels I ought to. We neither of us want to. But then we neither of us quite see how we –'

'Oh, *take* Batts if he offers. Much better let him do what he wants.'

She spoke decidedly and might well, he could see, have made an excellent wife – perhaps for Considine. She went on: 'I mean your work here isn't, is it? as interesting as it sounds. And it can't be necessary. I've known What's-his-name for years and he's never advanced anybody. I hear he thinks highly of you, but I'm not sure that is to be encouraged; he's been the coming man himself for too long.'

'I don't think I'm ambitious,' said Rodney. She guessed that he did not know what ambition meant. He had an idea of worth, virtue, a strong sense of England; he desired to advance something, not for himself, and consolidate something.

'Whereas at Batts?' she said.

'I should fruit farm. The present orchards are magnificent, though the apples are never got in in time; they rot in the grass. All the land's good, though it's never been developed. I should begin –'

'Oh, if you know what you'd do, I should consider that settled.'
Recollecting that she had offered him nothing to drink, she rang
the bell behind her.

Rodney's breath was taken away; the future did seem to have
adjusted itself. While he was busy with the syphon, she laughed.
'You can all be together for Christmases.' Batts had quite decided
her in his favour; the life would be perfect for Janet, the place
would be perfect for Janet's children. As for Edward, she thought
a good many children would do him good. At the thought of
grand-children, she and Considine both sprang up a generation in
stature. Though Rodney naturally could not realize how sadly
funny it was, her idea of Christmas. For the young Meggatts'
relatives would be an impossible combination; none of the
Studdarts or Tilneys would wish to meet Considine, few would for
long be easy under a roof with herself. This rueful contemplation
of fact, from time to time, was the nearest she ever came to
penitence.

Edward spending a family Christmas would hardly know himself. Her own family seldom 'gathered'; herself, she put up the
poorest show of festivity. She remembered one Christmas, their
last, in his little-boyhood, and the dumb ceremonial look they
exchanged, he and she, over a tinselled branch of the tree between
blue and pink rickety candles: she lighting the last. Edward,
polite from the cradle, had manifested surprise, though he had for
days been aware of her preparations – 'You shop,' he had said,
'while I look in the other direction.' Solitary in velvet, he had
attempted to group himself at the foot of the tree. Some tinsel
caught fire; for a second his small face had animated.

'What a lot of presents for one little boy,' he said as she cut
down the sixth. Considine had sent him a small stuffed bear that
stood by the tree, upright, with brown paper over its head. It was
a stuffed real bear, not jointed, not a teddy-bear; Edward, who
had wished for a teddy-bear, pulled at its limbs in silence. 'It's a
real bear, Edward.' 'I know it was once.' It was a dead bear now
and appalled him. Prey to this or some other obscure disappointment he soon afterwards wept and asked to be taken to bed early.
She had asked Considine not to come, so the evening with its
unescapable smell of wax, of charred tinsel, of crackers she had
had to pull with herself with both hands because he hated the
bang, remained dedicated to futility. She had perceived that

39

night – and the next, when she and Considine too rashly, too moodily met for her consolation – that any failure in pleasure is absolute . . . Indifference now drew a line of equality through those days. And she had since seen also, loving Edward from a distance candidly and with less alarm, that he had been a quite ordinary child.

No one had ever thanked Considine for the bear. She now denied herself sensibility, and was surprised when, from some odd angle, someone had once represented him to her as pathetic. As his good friend, however, the best she could wish him was constancy in his absences. *He* loved gatherings; his hospitality was notable. At Batts Considine would wish to assemble them all; Edward and pretty Laurel, the comfortable Studdarts. To his overbearing capriciousness difficulties would not present themselves. He forgot almost everything. Too plainly she saw the Studdarts perplexed, Edward stiffening; Laurel's bright head turned in repudiation. She did not care to think of Considine sentimentally wounded. To be rebuffed as an uncle would be disastrous.

'Will Considine come to your wedding?'

'We don't know; he's still in Greece –' Rodney broke off, wondering if she knew. 'Indeed?' she said. 'In love?' she wondered.

'We so seldom meet,' she said naturally. 'We meet by chance. There are so few coincidences.'

'Janet and I were a coincidence,' said Rodney with an engaging egotism. He was younger than she had, for the moment, realized. Then he ever so slightly blushed. For this unhappy mother of Edward's – now so contentedly tracing her cat's spine – was for himself and Janet a major, almost a tragic, coincidence. Bearing down, spectacular as an iceberg over the sunny waters of their engagement, she had so nearly wrecked them.

That night, they dined out late, hilariously: Lady Elfrida, Janet, Rodney, and Lewis Gibson whom they must meet. Janet had met him? That did not count, they must meet again. Lewis was Edward's best friend. He had understood Edward's mother perfectly from the first (better, he saw, than Edward) and often felt himself called up to interpret her. The Janet–Rodney development was after Lewis's own heart. Throughout dinner he disconcerted Janet by a kind, comprehending stare. At the wedding

40

he, the best man, had scarcely seen the bride's sister: both were abstractions. Now, she was a beautiful creature; in the Meredith tradition but mercifully almost utterly silent.

Lewis rang up Edward at midnight to tell him everything would be all right.

7

Lewis Gibson had a sister, Marise, at Mellyfield, who did not approve of new girls coming at half-term. Polite, she ignored Theodora with noticeable persistence. She was a bleak, fair girl with hair plaited back so tight that her eyes turned up at the corners. Theodora had, however, a certain advantage; she disliked almost everybody's appearance. She examined with irony the Second Eleven colours pinned to Marise's chest, her chapped hands that thawed less than half-way even in summer, her shoe from which a button was missing. Theodora was forced to take up a strong position from the very beginning; the first night she discovered that everyone else in her dormitory wore pyjamas. One of the girls had been nearly captured by brigands; one had travelled in Mexico; they all had brothers; none of them were interested in Switzerland.

They all undressed with their cubicle curtains undrawn, discussing Georgian poetry. When a bell rang they all drew their curtains and said their prayers, except one girl, an agnostic, who got into bed with a pious creak. Marise Gibson was head of the dormitory; when a second bell rang she said: 'Lights out,' because it was still June daylight. She said politely to Theodora in the next bed: 'I hope you are not homesick?'

'I have no home at present,' said Theodora.

'Oh – Excuse me, but we are always supposed to fold our clothes up.' Then she repeated, 'Lights out.' An honourable silence fell.

Theodora put out some interesting photographs on her dressing-table, but for some days no one looked at them. She put out silver brushes, but Marise said she must keep those in a bag. By day, Theodora was not overlooked. She broke her glasses at once and had to be moved to the front row, in algebra, to see the blackboard. She talked so much French in French class that Mademoiselle, unused for years to the language, was confused and became annoyed. In mid-morning break she played the Rachmaninoff prelude in C sharp minor loudly on the gymnasium piano till a mistress looked in to say it was break now and she had better go out and run about. At tea she sat down at the empty end of a table; a girl who was nice to new girls moved up and asked her about her home.

'I have no home, actually,' replied Theodora.

'Christine came this term too,' said the kind girl, nodding down the table. 'Her father is dead,' she added in a low voice. But Theodora had already distinguished the other new girls and learnt to avoid them.

She made her first impression on Jenna, who collected tortures. Theodora knew of two new ones, one Chinese, something to do with a rat, and one Italian, with weights. Jenna went green, became quite friendly and asked Theodora if she had ever been into a used vault. Neurosis had quite a high value at Mellyfield; the third night Theodora shrieked with confidence when a bat came into the dormitory. Two of her companions, Jane and Ludmilla, had a fixation about earwigs. Next day, in break, they asked her to walk with them round the garden. But they were 'younger ones'; Theodora, looking round in vain for Jenna, replied that she ought to go in and write letters.

'But we're not allowed to, in break; we're supposed to run about.'

'Where do you all run *to*?'

'We sit in the potting-shed mostly, but sometimes we let the guinea-pigs out and chase them. If they're not caught in time we get excused drill.' Finally, the three strolled down to the kitchen-garden and ate radishes. Theodora moved on and ate carrots, while the others looked on in alarm. 'My dear, you *must* have an inside!' Theodora went in to geometry with earth in her teeth.

'Theodora,' Miss Milford said plaintively, 'what do you keep sucking?'

'Please, I have earth in my teeth.'

'You had better go to the bathroom and wash your mouth out. ... Jenna, it is not amusing ... Hester, why need you poke Elizabeth? ... Theodora, can you go out *quietly*?'

Altogether, she created quite a pleasurable disturbance, and though Marise at the time did not move an eyelid she paused that evening to look at Theodora's photographs.

'Why,' she said, 'that's the *Tilney* wedding!'

'Oh yes. Why? Do you know them?'

'My brother was best man.'

'Oh, in spectacles; I remember. I didn't see you there.'

'Measles. Do you know the Tilneys well?'

'The Studdarts are my oldest friends.'

'Oh? I don't know them. Laurel seems quite pretty.'

'She's not really my type,' said Theodora. 'Janet has more personality; I'm devoted to *her*.'

Everyone listened. Theodora pulled off her stockings and threw them about casually. She did not seem to care if she went on. Marise, binding up tightly the end of her pigtail, remarked with authority: 'Lady Elfrida's difficult.'

'Oh, do you think so?'

'My brother doesn't at all,' Marise said quickly. 'He understands her. But most people do.'

'Understand her?'

'No,' said Marise crossly. At this point the bell rang and they all knelt down to say their prayers. They did not speak again of the wedding for some days. Marise asked Jenna not, in the public interest, to encourage Theodora. Jenna said she hadn't, she thought Theodora was quite mad.

'You do,' said Marise. 'You laugh at her. And look how she bucks about playing the violoncello. The one thing she oughtn't to be is taken notice of. She's been probably sent here to make nice friends. Jenna, I hope you won't mind my saying, but you do get in with the most awful people through talking horrors. Look at that Harris girl who had young men.'

'My dear, I don't mind telling you while we're on the subject; that girl had *the* most lurid mind. But you see, Marise, I'm terribly interested in human nature. But I shouldn't think Theodora had young men.'

'I should think she'd do anything to make an impression on anybody.'

The girls at Mellyfield developed very early a feeling for character. They were interested in their own personalities, which they displayed, discussed and altered. They were very much aware of each other and studied each other's profiles in chapel or during

43

concerts. They read psychology to each other on Sunday afternoons. Everyone knew, for instance, that Jenna's insincerity arose from a nervous opposition to circumstance; that Marise to live at all would have to break down her overpowering sense of order, that Hester since she was six had ruined all her friendships by her intolerance and that Ludmilla must be ignored when she squeaked at games because of a bad heredity.

So that Jenna (notoriously over-anxious to put herself in the right) resumed later to Marise: 'If we all can't bear Theodora it must be because she's aggressive, mustn't it? I mean it isn't as if she looked so awful, or smelled or anything, or were at all common. Now I do wonder *why* she –'

'She certainly is aggressive. She can't even do her hair without banging the things on her dressing-table about as though she were cooking.'

'Perhaps she's unhappy.'

'I don't suppose she's more unhappy than we are,' said Marise with some annoyance.

'But we at least do *know* we're unhappy.'

Marise, who saw where this was leading, said: 'Well, I don't think she need be asked about it her first term.'

'I do think she's got a good deal of personality,' said Jenna wistfully.

'Well, you try. You just have her in *your* dormitory. And besides, she snores.'

June was kind that year and Mellyfield beautiful. Classes gathered under the trees; girls, stepping in and out of the windows, crossed the lawns from shadow to shadow in fluttering red tunics; lime-flowers dropped on one's book in French. Theodora warmed a little to the spectacle. She distinguished herself as a young man in one of the Saturday night plays – these improvised, unrehearsed, in the manner of *commedie dell'arte*.

'You make a marvellous man,' said Jane and Ludmilla.

'Men walk with their elbows out, women walk with their elbows in,' vouchsafed Theodora. 'I was told that once and it makes all the difference.' She suggested that they should act Don Juan. Jenna, who was influential in these matters, was more than agreeable. She tied up her hair in ribbons over the temples like a Velazquez girl's. She had always known she had more passion than she could express. Tights gave out and the lords and attendants had to walk on in togas, but Miss Byng said the conception was excellent.

'How different you are with no spectacles,' said Doña Anna, lingering by the bathroom door.

'We've never had so much love in a play before,' said Hester, joining them. 'Generally, we just arrange for lovers to go off tenderly. I mean, I do think Theodora's extraordinary.'

'I suppose I can't imagine feeling self-conscious,' said Theodora, straddling a little.

'You tickle my ear when you kiss,' Doña Anna said thoughtfully. 'I do wish you'd hold your breath next time.' Marise, too thoroughly the Statue, was elsewhere, washing flour out of her ears. Doña Anna said casually: 'Let's walk round the garden before prayers.'

But next week, Miss Byng rather strongly suggested they should dramatize folk-songs. She said she liked their programmes to vary. So while Marise was excellent as a Spanish Captain, Theodora glowered in a smock. That night Marise said cheerfully in the dormitory:

'Lewis writes that Janet Suddart's engagement is broken off!'

Theodora put up a passionate opposition: 'I don't believe it!' Though she could not help thinking, 'This may be where I come in?'

'Well, ask someone yourself,' said Marise calmly. 'I should have thought you'd have heard, as you know her so well. Lewis says there's been some sort of trouble with the Tilneys.'

'That beastly Edward!'

'He's not; he's extremely sensitive.'

Marise understood Edward. Their relationship had been of the nicest; she had even thought, at one time, that when she herself had reached a gracious maturity and Edward had suffered a few years more they might well marry.

Theodora lay biting her nails in the moonlight. So Rodney, it seemed – as she feared, as she hoped – was not half a man. Next day, Sunday, she cut chapel and, making a guarded approach to the telephone, rang up Lady Elfrida. The Mellyfield Morris wallpapers were alert with daylight, but at Trevor Square morning had now only made a soft-footed entrance between the curtains and the telephone stung an intact silence.

'What is this I hear?'

45

'I can't think,' said Lady Elfrida from her pillows, blankly. 'And I am afraid I have no idea –'

'Mrs Alex Thirdman speaking,' said Theodora distinctly.

'Oh, how nice. But Janet has just gone home. Cheltenham six double-two something –'

'What about her engagement?'

'Oh? She has been engaged some time, you know. She has just motored home with Mr Gibson. He's wonderful, isn't he?'

'Who?'

'Mr Gibson. He had a long talk with Edward. I should contradict anything you hear.'

'I don't understand –'

'Oh dear, can I be the wrong number? Perhaps we're not talking about the same thing? Do forget what I said; I'm so sleepy – *Sixtus* – I'm so sorry, my cat is walking over my breakfast-tray – No, Sixtus, not in the grape-fruit. – Well, whatever we both mean, it's all quite all right, Mrs Thirdman. I have utter confidence in Rodney, haven't you? ... This has been so nice; we must meet again. We did meet, didn't we? Goo-ood-bye.'

She rang off pleasantly. Theodora, bruised a little about the initiative, was left contemplating the school wallpaper where orange-trees repeatedly sprang up and widely branched. She brought out her BB pencil and drew a bespectacled monkey, Lewis Gibson, swarming up one. Then she found the matron and said she feared her nose was bleeding, she had been unable to go to chapel. 'When it bleeds it bleeds torrents,' she said. 'One cannot tell how it may end. I thought I had better take no risks.' The matron sent her to lie down.

In reply to a letter, Janet wrote from Cheltenham:

DEAR THEODORA,

Thank you so much for your letter. I am sorry you worried, especially as you must be so busy and have important things to do. Everything has been all right and I was not unhappy, so please cheer up. I think Mr Gibson must have exaggerated a little without meaning to; he is so kind and anxious that everything should go off well. He takes so much trouble and even rang up Mother in the middle of the night to tell her not to be worried at me coming home next day. Please tell his sister how much my mother appreciated his kindness; she is so afraid she may have sounded irritable as she had been asleep. And please ask your mother not to worry. I cannot think what she can have heard; Lady Elfrida tells me

46

she rang up in such distress and did not seem herself at all. It was simply that there was a misunderstanding about my settlement. Father had wanted Edward to act as trustee and when the papers were half-way through Edward found he could not. So you see that was all. Laurel was rather worried and perhaps she exaggerated a little to Mr Gibson, who is so sympathetic.

But it is quite all right so please do not worry. Please do not not sleep, either! that must be awful; I always sleep so well. Rodney and I are to be married in October, as I think I told you. I hope you will all come. I expect you will like the Mellyfield girls more later on. People often do seem silly at first, especially many people. I am glad you like acting; yes, I should like to see you act sometime. It is kind of you to say you think about me; I am sure at a time like this one is glad to be wished luck. Did I say I would write? I am so sorry.

I have a great many presents to thank for, especially rugs and clocks. Uncle Considine is giving us a Bentley. I am afraid this is rather a stupid letter. It feels a very long letter for me to write.

Yours affectionately,
JANET.

P.S. – I quite agree with you about all music mistresses.

As term went on this letter, folded inside Theodora's camisole, became limper and limper until it entirely ceased to crackle. At last it fell out through the neck of her blouse while she turned a somersault on the horizontal bar. She exposed Lewis Gibson to his sister; she said *he* was what she would call officious. On the stairs at night she put Jenna right on the subject of love.

'No, you're wrong,' she said. 'It's something going on inside all the time like your stomach. Nothing makes any difference to it, not even the person.'

'But that would not be interesting, Theodora.'

Marise pointed out later that Theodora was not even correct. For surely even the stomach had intermissions between digestion?

8

A quarrel, a miserable affair, had for one day suspended Janet's engagement. Between herself and Rodney nothing was at fault. It was Edward who made an unfortunate entrance at Trevor Square, one evening forgotten by night when heat implacably closed, like glass, the open balcony windows. It was nine o'clock; he had been working late; and coming in to find Janet with his mother, could have sworn he interrupted a smile that was not for him. He sat down – but the place had never been home to him. Something about his manner drove his mother from the room, in unkind exaggeration of flight. She abandoned some peonies she had been settling in the Chinese bowl – she did everything, flowers themselves, at unnatural hours. The peonies dropped from the table; Edward went down on his knees to look for them among the furniture. Janet, standing in what remained of the light, said: 'Oh dear.' He was furious at her resignation.

'Why are we all in the dark?'

'I can't think – are we?' said Janet. They could see each other too plainly: it became obvious they were to quarrel. Edward, picking up the last of the peonies, said, too pleasantly: 'My mother is never alone, is she.'

'I shall be going home on Friday.'

'You misunderstand me –'

She knew she did not. 'How's Laurel?'

'Hating this heat.'

She may or may not have smiled, sitting there on the sofa mysteriously engaged with herself. 'But Tilneys,' continued Edward, 'generally seem to be overwrought. Did Rodney notice?'

'Rodney? Oh no, why? I think you exaggerate. I'll go to bed now, then you can talk to Lady Elfrida.'

'But it's nine o'clock.'

'Then I'll read.'

'But you don't read, do you?'

'I can,' said Janet, with an audible smile.

'You never ask what's the matter, do you? Perhaps you don't notice.'

'Well, I did think you were being a little odd. Are you tired, Edward?'

'Oh, no,' said Edward with irony. At home already he had reduced Laurel to tears. 'Why should I be tired?' He picked up a newspaper and staring at it in the dusk, went on in a raised level voice as though reading aloud: 'You see, Janet – or perhaps you may not see – things are being difficult at the best, and your attitude makes them impossible.'

'I didn't know I had an attitude,' said Janet, genuinely surprised.

Edward preserved an ironic silence.

'But, Edward, we really cannot quarrel. Please . . . Do think of what is convenient: we are relations for life. I mean, we shall stay with each other, shan't we, at Christmas and everything? It would be impossible for Laurel and me to be divided. For as long as we live, I suppose about fifty years, we shall all always be meeting and talking over arrangements. At least, that is how we have been brought up. You must see what families are; it's possible to be so ordinary; it's possible not to say such a lot. I didn't expect you'd want me to say I was sorry about the Meggatts; I thought that was all understood. I never can say things anyhow. Did you really think I was marrying into them to annoy you?'

'Why should I think you should want to annoy me?' returned Edward coldly. Feeling his way from switch to switch he turned on all the lights. He blinked; the darkness gone from the room seemed to inhabit him. Looking back at the moment afterwards, he seemed to himself to have suffered some distortion and to have thought of her as inflicting this. Standing back from the sofa, her implacable face with the downcast eyes his mark, he began: 'If you ever cared for him –'

Janet looked up.

'I hope,' she said, 'Laurel may never know you. You are like a malicious, horrible child.'

They both thought of the fifty years. Edward, from whom some dark but positive virtue seemed to have gone out, was deserted by feeling. 'You exaggerate,' he said tentatively. She could not dislike what had been said more than he did; he considered, however, that it was for her to speak. They must get back somehow. She, however, not looking again at him, allowed two clocks to tick and the last outgoing traffic – lorries, what sounded like a removal in furniture vans of entire London – to drag its slow iron chain down the Brompton Road. Either she was without mercy or she could think of nothing to say. Edward left the room and went home. As she refused to do even that for him he did not say good night.

His visit had been brief: Lady Elfrida, about to come down again, looked down with surprise from her bedroom landing at his

descending head. She, of course, reproached herself. The long
low little room, left alone with Janet, was mortally disconcerted;
the lamps staring. A room does not easily re-compose itself, laugh,
remark some inconsequence, remember a tune. Lady Elfrida
would have recovered herself almost at once. 'Gone?' she said,
coming in.

'He had to go,' said Janet.

Edward arrived home in desperation. The refractions of this
upon Laurel were endless but she did not dare weep again that
night. Next morning she came in a taxi to Janet and wept there.
'Janet, what can you have *said* to him?' She saw plainly that
Janet must be in the right, she was so hard. She implored Janet
to be kinder. At this point, Rodney was announced; Janet meeting him collectedly on the stairs broke off their engagement
provisionally. Rodney, seeing that she was not herself, said he
would come back at six and went away considerately. He knew
that girls, even Janet, had an emotional family life, but that he
and she would be married in October. Meanwhile, Lady Elfrida
could not be kept from her own drawing-room; it had to be
explained to her that Laurel did not know why she was weeping.
She said at once that Laurel must be going to have a baby.
Laurel repudiated the baby; Lady Elfrida said that at all events it
was wretched to be a woman and gave her two tickets for the
Ballet. A note from Edward to Janet arrived by special messenger.
He asked that nothing might be remembered; she wrote back:
'Naturally.' Three friends of Lady Elfrida's arrived for lunch. At
five o'clock Lewis Gibson appeared with his new car to ask Janet
to come for a turn round the Park. He found Janet packing. What
she would really like, she said, would be to be driven to Cheltenham, not today but tomorrow. Lewis vibrated with compre-
hension. Lady Elfrida detained him but he had time that night to
write to his sister at Mellyfield and telephone to Edward and Mrs
Studdart.

Next day, till Uxbridge she sat like a sad Holbein; at High
Wycombe he made her laugh, before Oxford she was cheerfully
looking about her. Afternoon light for years was stored on the
Cotswolds; Lewis, swerving along the taut ridge road, kept
offering his companion the horizons and the sky. Cheltenham,
white in trees, appeared grander than London; on the hills
around, villas tilted comfortably in their gardens at a deck-chair

angle were past amazement. Lewis thought of tea, Janet felt lighter for the birth of this positive grief.

At Corunna Lodge they found Rodney rolling the tennis court with her father. Some presents had come, and a longer letter from Edward who thought he must have been mad. Rodney kissed her and did not speak of yesterday – they were, of course, to marry. The garden was gauzy with midges; they had tea out of doors where the willow wept in a cheerful trickle against the sun. Lewis produced a good deal of laughter and Colonel Studdart, liking the young fellow, confessed he did not know where he should be without both his daughters. Lewis, who was composing a letter to Edward, replied earnestly: 'You must marry again.' Meanwhile Mrs Studdart and Janet opened the presents together, agreeing how nice it was that Rodney should like Lewis.

That afternoon leading on to July was mother to a succession; a personal calm set in and the weather remained equable. Nothing, when Janet looked back over the years for its reassurance, nothing of that afternoon remained particular but a picture of Lewis, crosslegged on the grass in a cloud of midges, polishing his spectacles on his knee. And the birth of a joke: whenever Colonel Studdart mislaid his detective story, choked or received no answer to a pre-paid telegram, he would make round eyes in imitation of Lewis and say: 'I must marry again.'

In August Rodney went up to Scotland and Janet accompanied her parents to Cornwall – it was easier to be apart. Returning, Rodney found September still ahead and a little terrible. Her trousseau was not complete. He stayed at Batts – the place was henceforth to command him – and came very little to Cheltenham. The young Tilneys, who could not leave London for long again so soon after Dalmatia, visited the Daubeneys in August for a long weekend.

In September, Laurel discovered she was going to have a baby. Resolving to keep the matter for as long as possible from Lady Elfrida, she attended the wedding with a sense of double importance. At the wedding, Lady Elfrida was very much present. It was she who helped Janet into the gold dress.

Part II
The Fine Week

I

Anna and Simon Tilney, crouching among the bushes, bit into the sharp green gooseberries that turned their palates to blotting-paper. They spat the gooseberries out again: this was just for sensation. Their cousin's great-uncle Considine, stretched between the low spiny branches, lay almost relaxed beside them. Between his head and the earth Anna had slipped a cabbage leaf. His hands, on the leaf, were clasped loosely under his head; one eye was closed, one glassy with light reflected the sky where a hawk swung and dropped a little. This hazy and close afternoon of Whitsunday the three had gathered without purpose in a remote quarter of Batts kitchen-garden. Considine was not fond of children but found himself perpetually among them. The Tilneys' young cousin Hermione Meggatt still hung about the stables, vainly calling them. It seemed curious that an only child should not have accustomed herself to solitude.

'It's too high,' Simon said impatiently of the hawk. 'You couldn't shoot it, even with a gun. Go on, please.'

Anna, gently prodding Considine in the ribs with the toe of her sandshoe, said: 'Yes, go on,' with equal authority. He had been telling them a story about a tiger.

'Well, the arm went gangrenous and had to be cut off. We had no anaesthetic ·'

'Gas, ether, chloroform,' explained Anna to Simon. 'Which hadn't you?' she said to Considine.

'We hadn't anything.'

'So then what did you do?'

'I took it off,' said Considine. The children hugged themselves, squatting lower. 'Does a black man's arm go blacker when it goes bad, or does it go blue? Describe.'

'I don't know that I could . . .'

'But haven't you ever seen a man quite eaten?' Simon said, dissatisfied.

Considine's reputation certainly did diminish. The Tilneys succeeded in laying bare large intervals of vacuity. They could not
imagine, obviously, what he really had done with his life: either
child could have lived it better on his behalf. 'So what did you
do *then*?' they kept asking. They had a strong feeling for continuity. Now he could not remember, for instance, what he had
done with the gangrened arm. Burned it? Buried it? Surely one
should remember burying an arm? Or if he gave it to somebody,
what did the man who took it away do then? His memory seemed
unnatural, he could not remember wondering or comparing, or
being at all surprised. His very tigers looked thin on this background of no-speculation.

'Well then, invent,' said Simon kindly. 'Tell us about an
imaginary tiger getting into a girls' school.'

'I'm asleep now,' said Considine, stung. In his time, he had
passed for a *raconteur*.

Simon himself was beginning a much better story about a tiger
when Anna jerked him down suddenly and put a hand on his
mouth. 'Here's Aunt Janet, and we are not playing with Hermione.'

But Janet was not concerned with her daughter's unpopularity.
She came down the path slowly, not wondering where anybody
was. She had counted back thirteen Whitsundays and was trying
to remember how she had spent the fourteenth. She had been
married ten years and was pleased by any recurrence, monotony
having already set up in her life its delicate rhythm. She
walked hatless in yellow linen under the veiled sky; her face was
clear to the children and Considine, who found nothing to read
there.

Janet, who went nowhere without purpose, had come out to
look at the gooseberries. The excellent tart at lunch had occasioned discussion. Rodney, who had by now his acres of
orchard, suffered rather than encouraged the extravagant kitchen-
garden and spared few of his men for it. Soft fruit for the house was
not plentiful. If from now on she were to feed her household on
gooseberry tart and gooseberry fool, as they desired, would any
be left to ripen in July when Laurel and Edward joined them?
Last year she had had new raspberry canes put in, but these also
seemed likely to disappoint her. It was difficult. Colonel Studdart
and Lewis Gibson were at Batts for this weekend; Mrs Studdart

had a bazaar coming on and could not leave Cheltenham. The Tilney children were here, convalescent from measles, to give Laurel a rest.

This present garden, her own, locked in high walls with its tradition of order, its Sunday silence, dissolved Janet's perspective of Whitsuns. Her thought – if it were thought – stopped. Looking closely along the gooseberry bushes she saw, between the bushes (she did not know how unwillingly), the Tilney children. The aunt in her took command.

'You'll get horrid pains.'

'We're spitting them all out again.'

'That seems silly, too,' said Janet. Considine, lying moveless under her no-comment, remained as the earth. He was not their aunt's affair. He and she could inhabit one house in intact solitude, unaware of those small obligations to speak or smile that make encounters tedious. They overlooked one another in perfect amity. Now she passed up and down the rows of bushes, lifting the low, heavy branches and stooping to look under them. The Tilneys, always surprised a little by life at the Abbey, felt that childhood here was certainly at a discount. Their Aunt Janet was not concerned with them. At home in Royal Avenue, everything the two children did had for their parents a poignant and charming importance. Edward and Laurel could hardly bear not to participate. Edward was always best pleased to discover them in the cellar or on the roof. The tabus of his own childhood had obtained for his children a system of rather paralysing unrestrictions. Their world which he believed himself constantly to inhabit was mysterious in Edward's imagination. From real affection and a shyness of asking for money the two never confessed that they would have preferred the rink or the riding-school to the afternoon twilight of Kensington Gardens, or tea taken to a band at the Trocadero to tea in the cave their father and mother built for them under the dining-room table. They secretly longed to play golf. Their Uncle Rodney spoke of making a links at the Abbey: they considered him perfectly adult.

'Are you looking for Hermione?' asked Anna helpfully.

'No.'

'We don't know where she is.'

'I expect she's quite happy,' said Janet. She pulled up some roots of groundsel and passed on: the afternoon had altered.

Anna returned her toe to Considine's ribs. 'Now go on,' she said. 'Tell us something that isn't about tigers.'

The white afternoon, undisturbed by wind or sunshine, undeepened personally by any hostility or attraction, hung gently, heavily over Batts. The large yellow stone house was quiet, with loud clocks. Rodney finished the *Observer* in the library, pressed the paper back into its folds and took it out to Colonel Studdart. He knew his father-in-law would have been glad of it sooner, but there were limits to hospitality. By this time, as it turned out, Colonel Studdart was asleep, his panama tipped over his eyes, in a wicker chaise-longue under the copper beech. Under the same maroon canopy another chaise-longue, empty, indicated an intention of Janet's. This quest of shade on a sunless day surprised Rodney, but Colonel Studdart's reasoning was faultless: you sat out only when it was hot, and when it was hot you sought a fine dark shadow. Colonel Studdart, to whom consciousness among all these cushions must have been pleasant, seemed sorry to have fallen asleep; a droop of incomplete resignation lengthened his chin. Sleep by day is seldom wholly dominant. Is it the misgivings of a journey but half accomplished that make the face of a daytime sleeper so uneasy, so remote from enlightenment that the whole range of waking sensibility lies between this and the triumphant serenity of the dead?

The Studdart practice of sitting out was in itself perplexing to Rodney, who had not known the sylvan deliciousness of a villa's garden or ever stared to infinity through a thicket of three hawthorns. He was a countryman. Pressed by the likeable family, Rodney sat out of doors (which became to him 'sitting about') with hardly more enjoyment or spontaneity than that with which he would have paddled or caravanned. With the duress and vigour of country life as his point of departure he took indoors his relaxations and was accustomed to view his fine trees, the dip of his grounds and the rise of his land from the library window. The seasons only turned him from hearth to window, window to hearth. Innocently, he associated this fancy of Colonel Studdart's with pine-woods, bus-routes, the proximity of a neo-Tudor gable and a portable gramophone. Nowadays, Janet never sat out unless someone desired her company. But if Colonel Studdart was pleased, Rodney was pleased also. And if Janet were unaccountable? He replied – he could not bear her to be away. Her absences, which he would hardly admit as absences, penetrated and racked him. Before death she had ghosts all over the house; she was preceded and followed. So that his library door was never quite shut, and more often than her movements explained he would look up for her shadow on the curved white wall of the stairs. Rodney did not miss Janet when he was out and about, but once in repose he became aware of a strong natural law: she should be by his side. Sometimes when she was dressing to go out he would catch at her hand that was going into a glove. Not always to kiss – simply he could not endure that first little departure.

So ten years had worked on a calm lover. He put the *Observer* down on the grass by the chair. Colonel Studdart groaned. Rodney returned to the library: she might soon be back from the garden.

But it was Hermione who looked round the door.

'Hullo, Father. I've been jumping off the mounting-block.'

'Good.'

'Fifty-three times, I did. You can imagine I'm blown.' She swung from the door-handle. 'Father . . .'

'Hermione?'

'Oh, all right . . . I suppose you'd like me to run along.'

'Why not look for Anna and Simon?'

'Oh, I see *them* quite a lot, thank you.' She was gone.

Hermione had been taught from infancy that she must not disturb her father; there was always, however, just a chance she might not be doing so, so she looked in frequently. Her grandfather, on his visits, seemed anxious to be disturbed and, had she known, Mr Gibson would have been glad of the same service.

Lewis Gibson was in the gunroom, trying to work. In his bedroom which, for all the perfection of its appointments, had been arranged with Janet's dear unintelligence, the writing-table was in the wrong place, and he could hear Hermione jump from the mounting-block twenty-nine out of the fifty-three times. A preposterous child for Janet. In the library there was Rodney, breathing – however quietly. Where he was now, in the gunroom, something seemed likely at any moment to clatter, to fall down. But under the best conditions Lewis never worked well in the country. In the morning he could not settle, towards the end of the morning he felt hungry, in the afternoon it was after lunch, after tea in summer he took exercise and in the evening he felt sleepy. So it became a mistake, from the point of view of ambition, to leave town at all.

On his return, however, he should have much to report. Affairs at Batts were of momentous interest to Lewis's circle. He would be able to assure Edward, Considine was now definitely to be out of England by July; he and Laurel might safely commit themselves to the visit. Apart from the exigencies of Whitehall, the times when Edward could visit at Batts were circumscribed. Naturally he must not meet Considine. Though he could not prevent his mother's going to Batts, her coincidence there with Considine had definitely been interdicted. He maintained a strong prejudice against Laurel's meeting Considine. (*She* would have ever so much to ask Lewis on his return.) At one time his children were not to be at Batts with Considine either, on any account. But since a first epidemic had swept the Tilney family, this had relaxed. He wished his children would not call Considine 'Uncle' and that Hermione Meggatt need not appropriate Lady Elfrida as 'Grandmother'. Between these whirlpools of sensibility, these reefs of umbrage, the two families had, however, steered for ten years an uneventful course.

Lewis felt that perhaps he ought not to work: Colonel Studdart was on his conscience. The old fellow was at a loss without his wife; the too calm household subdued his innocent bustle. Janet had all a busy woman's power of being nowhere. She had, it is true, given her father a spud with which he went diligently over her faultless lawns finding never a dandelion, not even a daisy. The Meggatts, uncle and nephew, though friendly were not affable; Edward's father-in-law had, moreover, with Considine a vague sense that something had once been regrettable. He found his Tilney grandchildren sincere, sensible, too polite; Hermione a tornado, without curiosity. So the old fellow returned to Lewis. They chatted. An unequivocal success of this kind, in any direction, was grateful to Lewis.

So Lewis got up several times and looked out of the window. But Colonel Studdart was still asleep ... At last, in despair, Lewis strolled out on to the terrace.

He yawned, drawing deep into his lungs the kind ennui. 'So here we all are,' he remarked (though they were none of them visible). He eyed the broad white afternoon; the horizon was

57

low, displacing only a little sky; the shrubberies from each side of the house ran out like arms. 'Well in . . .' said Lewis. (He meant: into life, and spoke for them all, from the early thirties; timed, approximately, with the season and afternoon.) 'Getting along nicely,' he added.

Now the scene, below, had a moving figure. Janet came out from the trees in the direction of the garden, to sit with her father. But he was still asleep, he did not even groan; she was nonplussed. Here she was, quite thrown back on herself – she did not look up at the house. Lewis wondered what she would do. In the dark shade of the beech she remained upright, oblivious sentinel of oblivion, a little behind his chair. Her hand moved slowly over the chair-back, not touching the wicker, moulding the air above; she did not quite smile. So, intimate, she could have been. In proximity to the beloved one caresses the chair – in speaking or not speaking – the curtain, or else the grass, the tree-trunk, glad of texture that electrifies curiously to the touch. What passed under her fingers now?

Evidently she had forgotten Colonel Studdart.

Some telescope brought her up to Lewis's eye, distinct but unforgettably distant. His view of her was unique: he could not account for this. Then he understood; solitude is in its nature invisible; he had never looked for so long at anyone who was alone.

2

Lewis's sister Marise was at present in the Tyrol with her fierce friend Theodora. With regret, he saw little of Marise at any time. At twenty-six she was aloof, important, with a cool little air of sufficiency that discredited marriage: she could command from any quarter a temperate admiration. She lived in a flat with Theodora, off Ebury Street. The claims of this rather neutral friendship of Theodora's were a relief to Mr and Mrs Thirdman, who enjoyed without any disturbance their cottage in Sussex. They rallied, in fact, to something a little beyond them when, on infrequent Sundays, the composed profiles of the two young women slid past the cottage windows and the car turned with precision in at the small yard gate.

Theodora no longer bullied her parents – they had, perhaps, the slightest possible sense of a deprivation – her energies flowed out in other directions now. It was hard to know what to talk to the girls about; they were tall and seemed oppressed by the low ceilings. They preferred, however, standing to sitting, and had, while Mr and Mrs Thirdman anxiously talked, the air of reserving their judgement. Their professions remained above discussion; they did not care for the theatre, did not have friends who married. . . . 'And Theodora, who have you been meeting?' 'Well – really, Mother, it would be difficult to explain.' Theodora was handsome now (they had it on good authority), still big-boned, still arrogant, still short-sighted. She saw little, but regretted, you could be certain, little that she had missed.

Once the girls had brought Lewis, who did sit down and was most reassuring. The Thirdmans' family life became natural at once; they had feared sometimes it must be exceptional. And Lewis's life was full of small difficulties he seemed glad to discuss. As to his friends – he was indiscreet winningly. He opened vistas of speculation down which the Thirdmans delightedly wavered. They had had no idea, for instance, that Edward was difficult . . . They could not have said Lewis gossiped, but they did feel he would have been a more natural friend for the daughter they might have had. They asked him to come again, and heard years afterwards from the Studdarts that he had still a lively intention of so doing.

This Whitsuntide there could be of course no question of any reunion, since Theodora and Marise were in the Tyrol. The Thirdmans spent Whitsun happily in their garden, an island between the roaring bus-routes. But Lewis at Batts grew melancholy, for some reason, as the Sunday drew out. Tea did not cure him, and the church bells made further inroads on his composure. He felt he had no attachments.

Now dinner was over, the cool May night, scentless, stood along the tall windows all half open. Far down the drawing-room a fire of beech, a fanciful summer fire lit for the eye, orientated the party. Nothing was said, and as nothing but Lewis's melancholy remained unspoken the lamplit air of the room was like still, clear water.

Janet came from the fire and halted, for no reason, where Lewis leaned on the window, his elbow along the sash.

'Well . . .' said Lewis.

'I believe it's cold,' said Janet, and stretched out of doors a bare inquiring arm.

Lewis took the remark as confidential. 'Would you like me to shut the window?'

'It's just that Considine . . .' She followed with her eye the line of a possible draught from the window to the back of Considine's neck. Lewis shut the window. 'Such a nice day,' he added, looking back regretfully for all he had missed.

She smiled, pleased: the day here was her own. He sighed, but as his happiness was on record she did not endeavour to understand him. She took little account of variations in Lewis – or for that matter, in anyone. 'Come back to the fire.'

But Lewis said confidentially: 'Hermione tells me she jumped off the mounting-block sixty-nine times. Do you think that can be good for her inside?'

'Fifty-three – I don't know, Lewis; she's so independent. I can't keep forcing Anna and her together. And Simon and she fight.'

'Those are interesting children,' said Lewis, who did not care for the Tilneys.

'They are, aren't they,' agreed Janet, without interest. 'I must say, they're devoted to Considine.'

'Does Edward mind?'

'I've no idea,' said Janet. 'I don't think he knows.'

'How do you think Edward *is*?' said Lewis, leaning back against the shutter luxuriously.

'I haven't seen him for more than a moment for nearly a year. He took me out to lunch before the Flower Show. He told me he had been speculating a little. I said I was so glad. Is he still?'

'Very cautiously,' replied Lewis.

'Well, he ought to be cautious,' said Janet, thinking of Laurel. 'Lady Elfrida, you know, speculates too fearfully.'

Janet did not take this in. 'I haven't seen Laurel since Easter,' she continued. 'It will be nice when she and Edward are here in July. I thought we might all –'

But at this point Rodney turned from the fire to look for Janet. Why should she have a fire lit for them all, then stand by the window? Followed by Lewis she returned to the sofa and sat down. Her husband, her father, her husband's uncle all sat down, with an air of having gained their point. 'I was saying,' she told them, 'that in July, when Laurel and Edward are here, we might all . . .' But Lewis remembered a look, an equally even and dark look, that, leaving the window, she had exchanged with the night.

They had exaggerated, however, Hermione's independence. 'Ho!' Janet's daughter exclaimed, upstairs, at about half-past nine, and as Anna took no notice repeated the challenge. The little girls were sleeping together.

'Wazzat?' asked Anna. Then she sat up, alert. But the house once again was not on fire. Nothing had stopped, either; she could hear a train round off its curve of sound in the hollow distance. The night was fixed: she just saw the windows, Hermione's low little oval mirror. The white glossy curtains moved now and then, like someone taking a step forward then standing still. Anna had heard of fear but marvelled at it. She sat up now to stare, vigorous as a crocus in her little sheath of assurance.

'What *do* you want, Hermione?'

Hermione explained that Anna had been asleep. Anna said, No; she was just lying.

'Well, you lie very flat,' said Hermione. 'Do you miss the traffic?'

'We don't have traffic where *we* live.'

'But I thought in London . . .' persisted Hermione.

'Well, we don't. Neither does our grandmother.'

'Oh, I've stayed with *her*. When shall I come and stay with you, Anna?'

'Mother says you're too accustomed to nannies.'

Criticism second-hand was distasteful to Hermione, as to any of us. 'I don't have nannies,' she said hotly. 'I have a maid, she's Swiss and I'm not accustomed to her. Then what did Uncle Edward say?'

'*I* don't know,' replied Anna, bored. 'I don't suppose he said anything.'

'Then what did Grandmother say?'

'She's not your grandmother, Hermione; she's not even your aunt. You can't have *everybody* you know.' Anna was quite right in thinking Hermione spoilt. Unfortunately she went on for too long. 'I never heard of anybody like you, Hermione, wanting to have everybody and everything. I tell you I never heard . . .'

'*I* don't want anybody's old grandmother!'

'But you love her,' said Anna, shocked.

'I don't want anybody's old cousins either,' went on Hermione wildly, thumping her pillow in the dark.

Lady Elfrida had said she did not see how a Meggatt could possibly be so excitable. Janet could not account for this either. At Trevor Square, Hermione had stampeded the Siamese, screamed in Harrod's (she thought she was lost), screamed at Maskelyne and Devant's (not a fortunate choice of Lady Elfrida's) and when she was left at home played Jezebel with a teddy-bear on the balcony, attracting a small crowd. Lady Elfrida found herself quite annoyed, and was surprised till she recollected Edward. For here she was in charge of a highly-strung child again: something-or-other about cycles . . . But Edward's excitement had been ingrowing.

Miniatures of the two little girls hung on a plaque in Lady Elfrida's bedroom, with Simon's above them. Simon could be left out of any discussion, he was a pure Studdart with a square head like his grandfather's. (Disappointing: Laurel had passed on worth but not distinction.) Whereas Anna Tilney had quite a touch of her Aunt Janet's distinction – not Edward's – a fine pale little gloomy face, just so curved at the jaw and temples as to escape squareness. *She*, however, might have had no eyelids, she never looked down. Her look, which was uncomplex, attached itself to an object with almost passionate rationality. She was fair, like Laurel, and would have been a suitable daughter for Rodney. She embarrassed Lady Elfrida and put even Mrs Studdart constantly in the wrong, for she was a born granddaughter.

Finally, Hermione was fair, ash-blonde – there was to be no variety – with the inevitable Meggatt chin. Her eyes, red-brown like the flesh of a prune, were set too near in, too deeply, over her high-bridged nose with its arched nostrils. Her look flickered, darted, and when it wanted to fix an object stole on it sideways – feverish child of Janet's. When she was tired her eyes had a very slight cast. In vain did her mother take her to the oculist. She looked an excitable little liar and sometimes lied.

'Well, I can't help it, Janet,' said Lady Elfrida tactlessly, after a third return from the oculist's. 'You should have had dark children. Apparently she's not even short-sighted; I'm certain she doesn't live in a world of her own. I don't know what you're to do.' She would have been sorry, however, to have missed Considine's great-niece.

— This in parenthesis — At present Anna, annoyed, had turned on the light and was getting out of bed without a word. Hermione understood that this was awful.

'Where are you going?' she asked humbly.

'In to Simon.'

'Oh, Anna, listen; do stop, Anna! I'll tell you a secret idea.'

'Simon and I have got secret ideas, thank you,' said Anna coldly. This was likely to happen to Hermione throughout life; she was more unfortunate than she knew.

'Listen — I'll call her my un-grandmother, and you shall call him your un-great uncle?'

'He's the same relation to us whatever we call him.' But Anna did so far relent as to sit on the side of her bed, still with the light on. (As a matter of fact, Simon bored her.) She swung her strong little feet and curled her toes. A Good Shepherd that had been Janet's looked down at both lambs with an impartial sweetness. Yet Anna had throughout an almost divine advantage. Hermione made a desperate effort to entertain her.

'How long,' she said, 'is the longest you've been in a train?'

'Sixteen hours.'

'Oh, Anna . . .'

Naturally, Anna had travelled. Already she was in a position to disparage two or three places abroad. She drew her feet grandly under the bedclothes. The coloured blanket was prettier than anything she had at home; she understood that the Meggatts were fortunate but in some way deplorable. 'You're sick in trains, aren't you?' she said more kindly. She picked her pillow up by the frill and thumped it out.

The door opened: Janet, in the doorway, told herself this was shocking. She knew children ought not to talk with the light on at ten o'clock. There was nothing a child need say at that hour — she wished her own day ran in as brief cycles.

'You two, do you know what time it is? I think you must be crazy.'

'Father reads to me if I can't sleep,' said Anna promptly.

'Does he? Well, here you have to go to sleep by yourselves,' said Janet. As Anna was not her child, she sat down on Anna's bed and looked at her kindly. They should have known each other. 'Count sheep,' she suggested.

'I can't count sheep I don't see.'

63

Janet sympathized. 'And don't,' she added, 'let Hermione talk again.'

'*Mother . . .*'

'No, Hermione; I'm annoyed.' Janet stroked back Anna's hair and kissed her: alas, no fair little girl would ever be gay like Laurel. Was something drying up at the source? And why, meanwhile, was Hermione looking up at the high mild ceiling? She lay, so still, with that black moral line all round her; a bad little girl. Janet tucked Anna's pink blankets in with a tenderness not for Anna. She turned out the light and crossed to the other bed.

Hermione's face came up in the dark, her arms, her whole body. She whispered: 'You do love me? You do really love *me*?'

Janet knelt with her face on the pillow. 'That is a secret.'

'So much that it is a secret?'

'You're my treasure.'

'Mother, you smell so lovely, I'd like to eat you . . . More than anyone in the world?'

Not far off, Anna lay listening in vain in the new, close darkness; waiting for Janet to disengage herself from Hermione's arms.

3

On Whit-Monday the clouds gathered; Tuesday was wet. Janet drove her father and Lewis to the station. Simon came too, to buy Seccotine; he sat in the back of the car with his grandfather: two half-crowns changed hands more or less silently towards the end of the drive. Simon leaned forward to ask whether, this being so, he might buy a saw. Janet did not hear: the loud rush of the car through puddles also made some of Lewis's talk inaudible. Eyes fixed on the streaming windscreen, she heard him remark that summer had died young and, later, was this not like a wedding day?

'Whose?'

'Anyone's.'

'Ours was fine,' said Janet.

Lewis, looking intelligently through the rain, made some remark about the village of Batts Monachorum, to which she did not attend. She remembered, on the way back she must call with that message at the rectory, and at the station she must find out if the weedkiller had arrived yet and possibly make a fuss. 'I wish,' she said, 'we lived on the main line.'

'Why?' said Lewis, starting violently. 'It doesn't matter,' he added, with reference to his own journey, though there was nothing he hated more than a rural junction. 'I mean,' he said, 'it doesn't matter to me.' He suspected yesterday, from her more than normal preoccupation, that she suspected herself of having said too much – somehow, sometime, about somebody; perhaps on Sunday night. He had been at pains ever since to correct the impression. Now she was frowning at some difficulty.

'If you really have that quarter of an hour at Doddington Junction, could you inquire about a parcel for me at the goods office? Could you really, Lewis? It would be so kind. It ought to have been delivered on Saturday. I think it's been hung up.'

'That must be difficult for you,' said Lewis earnestly. 'I suppose I shan't see you again for a long time?'

'I may come up to Trevor Square for a few days.' She turned the car up the station approach, past the white palings; they splashed through the tarry puddles. Janet waved to somebody. Then: 'Simon,' she called back, 'look after Grandfather's rug and his magazines.' Colonel Studdart was to have quite a send-off, but Lewis felt he had already departed. 'It's been so nice,' he said, like a ghost, getting out.

'It's been so nice,' agreed Janet, looking up at the station clock.

Simon was not sorry to see the last of the visitors; he had a busy day before him. He glanced once at the engine, then returned to the car, where, in the front seat, he sat turning his half-crowns over and kicking the gear gently. Then his Aunt Janet drove off rapidly; water went up in wings from some deep puddles. In the village he bought some Seccotine and bespoke a saw that cost seven-and-six. Perhaps Uncle Considine . . . perhaps even Uncle Rodney . . . Simon would tell them about the saw.

The rector's wife said to Janet: 'You had quite a party for Whitsuntide,' and Janet could not help feeling proud: they had filled two pews, with, on the outside, Considine himself, rigidly carved as a pew-end, leaning a little forward during the prayers and groaning into his hat.

'All gone?' said the rector's wife, looking into the car.

'All,' said Simon, 'except Anna and me.' The rector's wife laughed and invited the little people to tea. She nodded, and picked her way back up the wet garden path so cheerfully, anyone might have envied her. Janet, starting the car, did for a moment ask . . . Yet the rectory windows were Gothic, dark and pointed; the rector's eye seldom kindled; he was much alone with theology, half into his roll-top desk. A poor companion, even to his Maker.

Today this surely was the wettest village in the world: the poor late lilac was sodden; its leaves ran like gutters. Rain fell over dark doorways; the plaster cottages were distraught with it; the brick cottages sullen. Smoke from the dinner fires hung heavy, clotting the trees, and where under dark eaves the old woman still did not die, geraniums stifled, pressing close to the panes. The International Stores, full of cocoa, stood over its red reflection. No one crossed the street or even came to a door: a quenched, drenched day, thought Janet. And in the village, something suspended, perhaps finally over: evening brightly dissolving the roofs, the hourless blank of sunshine, dark lamplight, the bucket swinging up bright from the cold well. There would be worse days here, some better; none, you had to believe, final. To be consoled it was better to live indoors, without spectacle.

Meanwhile, Simon was anxious to be at home with the Seccotine.

At the Abbey, coming out nonchalantly between the hall pillars, Considine met them without interest. After breakfast she had seen him go out with Rodney, collars up, looks contracted, into the slant of rain. Here, however, he was once more: notably disengaged. 'This will go on,' he said, indicating the weather. 'Your husband likes it.' He helped her off with her coat.

Considine was not so tall as his nephew; he was slighter, steeper about the cheek and narrower at the temple. As Rodney gained in maturity, Considine receded to a second, happier adolescence. Mutual esteem contracted to a small, pure nugget, unfruitful as metal. Irony became apparent in Considine's manner, forbearance in Rodney's. These last four weeks it became palpable: Considine was once more due to be out of England. This affair here at Batts, this existence, did not seem, clearly, much of an affair to Considine. His courtesy, his loyalty to herself (from this most abrupt of friends and careless of lovers) bore in strongly upon

Janet that she was not his type. The plain fare of their daily companionship was Lenten (with Easter always ahead) to this uncomplaining sinner. She was, however, a fine woman; he had a keen sense of her quality. For her part, she resented a little on Rodney's behalf that too generous smile, that never visible shrug at their routine, their orchards . . . Here you had the most admirable of sober nephews, admirably rewarded.

'Quiet again now, aren't we,' said Considine, in civil reference to her guests' departure.

For himself, of course, the party had not been amusing. It was to be regretted there was no lady among them. Before the days of Rodney, Considine had been the gayest, the most unfaithful lover of his home. Batts had known flowery intermissions. Rooms long dark were unshuttered to daylight and animation; mirrors barely wiped clear of their film reflected a galaxy. Extravagant skirts brushed the lawns not then innocent of a daisy, parasols tilted this way and that on the landscape corollas of sunny silk. Country life was less rigorous, less professional; darkness came in early; legislation had not affected a summer day's accents; candles flattered the décolletage even at midsummer; one laughed late. A week fled, even a fortnight; then the looking-glasses were sheeted still with a smile in them; shutters went up again on the last of a gaiety that had tradition but no heirs . . . Janet thought she must have missed the true Considine, hardly met him; she had not seen his charm in play.

He regretted, she thought, no one. They were all scattered, tarnished, unwillingly dead. He was, however, deprived . . . 'Perhaps,' Lewis had suggested, 'we do not enjoy ourselves.' Perhaps one knew fewer ladies, perhaps they were less agreeable. In talk there appeared an asexuality, a competitiveness. Janet did not even know what Lewis meant; she supposed many women had always been dull. She would have invited anyone likely to entertain Considine! she could not think of anyone to invite. It was fortunate, she considered, that he was fond of children.

He was not fond of children. Simon bored him, the manly little fellow. Anna was, of course, a woman in embryo. But Hermione, had she indeed been Elfrida's granddaughter instead of his own niece, might have been said to show a touch of her grandmother's spirit.

Though Elfrida's had been a hard spirit. She had not, by any account, treated Considine well. Her silence from any reproach had, at the time of the *débâcle*, been cruelly positive; in itself a wound for him. Fresh from the break-up in her life, that scandalous light only shifting from her a little, she had countered any approach from him, forbidding tenderness by her discernment, by her lucidity like an untouched girl's. He might never have moved her. It remained impossible for him, now as then, to tell at what point he had committed himself to failure. She undid passion. By an ironic denial in every look, every word, every letter that they each now needed the other for reassurance, she made it impossible for him to be at her side where, since the *débâcle*, the world looked for him. Legally accurate on the plane of emotion, she made out an over-good case for his instability. Having now only him, she sent him away finally. She had perhaps injured him, perhaps even vitally. Then she had persistently sought the light man in him, match for her light woman. Under her dry-eyed farewell look, her last tragic un-regret, in Paris, he had certainly desiccated. Leaving Europe, he left behind with her in that cold apartment, where she had created out of a dire intimacy with her surroundings, as in a sick-room, an icy but very real hearth, the whole spring of his being, a manhood she had demanded then undone. His active life, since its entire divorce from conviction, became spectacular; fame quenched notoriety, reputation succeeded rumour; she might have been said to have 'made' him ... It appeared, nowadays, natural that they should not have married; their separation took on the prestige of an old alliance. Some retreat of prejudice had permitted her to repair her own honour. Yet Considine lived and apparently flourished, as Edward's father, more notably sinned against, had broken-hearted declined and died: her victim.

So at Batts, for Rodney and Janet he remained a problem, an unmatched figure hardly sterner than in porcelain, lacking its pair. Their own world was smallish, equable and domestic; for Considine's entertainment they could think of no one but Elfrida. Again and again – with an eye to Edward – they had rejected the proposition; always with less fervour. Today (it was to be memorable) this rainy Tuesday, because he tapped the weather-glass, because he helped Janet off with her coat sighing, because her guests who had gone had not amused him, the portentous structure of this refusal quietly came down. It had been for years

. a shell. Today proved to be one of those weekdays, vacant, utterly without character, when some moral fort of a lifetime is abandoned calmly, almost idly, without the slightest assault from circumstance. So religions are changed, celibacy relinquished, marriages broken up, or there occurs a first large breach with personal honour. Rodney and Janet suddenly saw no reason why Elfrida should not visit at Batts with Considine.

About five o'clock, in a premature twilight, when the children had already begun to quarrel and come out one by one from the schoolroom with Seccotine on their hands, the afternoon post came in. Lady Elfrida wrote, proposing herself for Saturday. 'It's a pity she cannot come,' Janet thought immediately. She re-read the letter and summarized it for Rodney. 'Her cook's ill; she wants to shut up her house.'

'And she would like to see you,' said Rodney, 'but naturally she does not say so.' He liked the woman. And because there was more rain than even Rodney desired, because Janet, Elfrida's friend, looked more deprived than she knew and Considine rasped him (that yawn, feline, like one of his own masks!), Edward's tabu all of a sudden became intolerable. Rodney no longer regretted that he did not like Edward better. 'I can see no reason,' he said, 'why she should not come.' Passing his cup across for more tea he added: 'At any rate, *I* want her.'

'But we can't ask Considine to go?' said Janet quickly,

'Naturally not.'

'So they'll both be . . . ?'

'Why not?'

'But then Edward . . .'

'I really can't see . . .'

'No, neither can I, Rodney. But then . . .'

'I'm sorry for Edward, but life has really got to be lived somehow – Never mind if it's overdrawn, Janet; I only want half a cup; water it down.'

Janet tilted the kettle. Rodney so seldom spoke of Life that, surprised, she poured herself out a cup she did not want. 'But then Laurel may feel she ought to take the children away.' She and Rodney considered the possibility. But they could not help knowing the Tilney children were, in their parents' view, only too well where they were.

Lady Elfrida's coming occasioned little disturbance. Considine liked the idea. She was to succeed Colonel Studdart in the Four-poster Room at the head of the stairs; a housemaid re-lined the large presses. Hermione set out to finish a pen-wiper against time.

'No one wipes pens nowadays,' remarked Anna. 'Bags I do the flowers.' Hermione was setting in early to be the daughter at home. She made pen-wipers, hair-tidies and lavender bags she forgot to fill. She came alive socially twice a year, at the Nursing Fête and the Church Bazaar, where she sold little wilting bouquets, helped with raffles and relieved the stallholders. No one asked anyone else what they thought of Elfrida's coming; she appeared, like some unearthly bright visitant, to glide, to plane bird-like across the sky of the week, in their full view, soon to alight, above all discussion, upon the rising pinnacle of Saturday. She produced confidences and estrangements, like a ghost rumoured, perhaps seen.

Edward wrote seldom to Janet, he did not write now. It was Laurel who concluded:

'. . . and angelic of you to give Anna those pink smocks. She wrote Edward a great description of tea at the rectory; I think she is naturally funny, don't you? Of course we have never forced this or shown her anything "comic".

'Of course you must do what you think about Elfrida. Of course you are quite right to agree with Rodney. I'm certain a change will do her good. She came round here the other day looking like death and *kept* her taxi for three-quarters of an hour. You must not mind if it seems to us as though there had been an earthquake. Because it does rather. Edward is not asking about anything, so please do not ask about Edward. He's terribly tired this summer and I just don't think he can cope with any-thing more. If it is difficult about the children, will you send them home? I will be ready for them any day you wire. Of course, though, they would be terribly disappointed.

'(Man come about the carpets.)

'I don't think I feel so much as though there had been an earthquake, but as though I should never see you, or you would be different, or it would never be July. Funny to think I thought our carpets would never fade enough. The man just now was horrid and said of course I didn't expect cleaning to bring the pile up, did I? Of course I did. Why else should cleaning be so expensive? I expect he wanted to sell me a carpet, don't you? But, oh well, I hope you'll all be happy at Batts – Forgive me, Janet; I expect in a house like yours one has more of an outlook. But I do feel a bit like the carpets. Now I am going to Ranelagh with the Coutts.

'It's no use asking me what Edward feels about this because *I don't*
- *know*. I am having the red georgette done up, with a bolero. But Mrs
Coutts is a fearfully faded blonde: we all do – Oh, if Simon and Anna do
seem to quarrel, just say something funny and make them laugh. That's
what I always do. But they don't quarrel really. By the way, they say
Hermione sacrifices her teddy-bears; do you think she ought to?

'Janet, I'm not angry really; I can't help how I seem, London's so hot.
I wish I had lawns and lawns – Well, you'd feel the same way if it were
Rodney, wouldn't you?

'Anyhow, I should think you'd rather *not* know how Edward feels, as
you're committed?'

'It's hot in London, Laurel says,' said Janet, folding this letter.
She always had to cover Laurel a little; Rodney was juster to her
than was just. 'Edward says nothing,' she added.

Considine was already a new man. Heavy dews fell, the glass
moved to Set Fair, the present relaxed its grip on the house. Considine talked louder, expanded personally, took on an edge. Even
Janet became a woman to him; he remarked her slowness, her
beautiful limbs, her heavy eyes, her decorum. He understood
Rodney and thought of the two as lovers. It was today triumphantly Saturday, a hot blade of sunshine: Elfrida would be with
them by teatime. Without reflection, Considine anticipated her
coming.

4

Lady Elfrida, wearing a large bright hat, went down slope by
slope to the lake where, walking carefully on the slippery grass,
she skirted the water. The lake, bending round the contour of the
rise, had a rushing sluice at each end; the stream released from
artifice went its way in curves through the shallow valley with a
glad air of being its narrow self again. Over these flat meadows,
pricked with budding flags and dark orchises, and over the mild
ascent beyond, hung the whole bloom of June. Sky and earth
married in light; blue on the trees and grass, a gold obscurity, like
pollen, over the sky. It was very hot. But the lake, banked
steeply round and the banks shadily planted, had a scene of its
own; it was not exposed to the countryside. Pre-Tudor in origin,
at one time the Abbey fish pond, it had now the charm, the gloom,

the disassociation from use of a more recent polite century that had rebuilt the house and isolated a belvedere in Rodney's orchards. Here Hermione fished, but though a few carp still moved darkly they were unaware of Hermione's dangling pin. In despair, she had here abandoned the punt, adrift.

Lady Elfrida, not finding anyone here, looked at the lake. She had in her unreflecting view, with the dark water, Edward's annoyance – or chagrin? Had she done wrong? But no sense of delinquency shadowed her visit; she could not regret having come. Unaware that her coming had tipped a delicate balance, she delighted in what she had found. They were 'in form'; the days had been dignified by a state of high amusement. Elfrida, who forgot herself easily, forgot herself here. Fervent in her deprecation of the scandalous (as agonizing) she was innocent and, like a woman in whom the sense of dress is deficient, had to refer any standard of the becoming constantly to her friends. At Batts they seemed to think there was nothing wrong. To be once more with Considine was delightful; he took on as much, in her view, from this domestic setting as he did in Janet's from the social heightening and brightening Elfrida's presence set up. In London, lunching or dining with Considine at those intervals of a year or so, she was oppressed by a sad conventionality in their attitude. But here they discovered a new spontaneity; she could only vaguely suppose they had once been mistaken.

It was in the early mornings, or mornings for her early – when Edward's children advanced to her bed with propriety, following in the breakfast-tray, and Considine's great-niece, marking the further degree in relationship, hung like a hopeful sparrow about the door – that the for herself so fatal distinction between kinship and affinity was borne in most strongly upon Elfrida. At that hour conscience lies with the body supine, tenderly relaxed. And the clean young Tilneys standing along her bedside reproduced most strongly at that hour the whole family faculty for disapproval. She had certainly sinned, if only in lying now in her lace Dutch cap in a stream of mature sunshine, in seeking first the financial page of *The Times* (she speculated) or in refusing – contrary, she believed they believed, to the practice of grandmothers, – an egg for her breakfast. Meanwhile the young Meggatt haunted her dressing-table, explored her cosmetics and, without reproach for the omission, put away her pearls.

Yesterday had seen still another arrival at Batts. Elfrida and Considine, both out to evade Theodora, had today a quite new sense of complicity. Avoiding the skyline, swerving away from windows (the terrace was dangerous), stepping quickly back into trees or down banks, they had, alas, missed even each other. But at this point Considine came cheerfully, cautiously, down to the lake, signalling an 'all clear'. Once more they were thrown together.

Theodora's arrival had disconcerted them all a little. She had telegraphed her intention from Dover and, picking up her car in London, had been with them, as she had promised, about half-way through dinner, effectively checking the meal's rhythm. The downstairs machinery after the faintest possible jar reversed itself and began to produce soup again. The Meggatts' attitude to Theodora was fatalistic. She was again to be with them. Marise and she, in whom a change of mind would be inadmissible, sometimes revoked a decision with calm certainty. So that, although they were not 'artistic', you never knew where they might not be. This time a breakdown of plans, a break-up of weather in the Tyrol, had disgraced the Tyrol for them. They returned to England without warning, repudiating the Continent. Their flat was let; Marise imposed herself on her club though there was not a room vacant; Theodora telegraphed to Batts that she would be coming. It was important for her, also, to see Janet.

At Batts, Theodora was not surprised by the party's composition. Surprise does, of course, imply interest: whatever she lacked she civilly did not show it. Beyond calling Edward Maisie, she had at no time seemed to take any account of the Tilney problem. Sitting down to dinner, impassible in her dark coat and skirt, she glanced at the company casually, superciliously – Elfrida's damaged beauty, Considine's dry polish – like someone's notable tame panther loaned with its cage for the afternoon to a village entertainment.

'I expected,' she said to Janet, who took on the charmed air of someone finally singled out, 'to be abroad for at least another fortnight.'

'That seemed too good to be true,' said Rodney pleasantly. They were on these terms. While Considine asked himself: 'Where did I hear that charming voice before?' He had forgotten, before ceasing to regret, Lady Hunter Jervois.

73

'Yet here I am,' resumed Theodora to Janet. Here she and Janet were in fact – after the very slight effort it took to discount Rodney and all the others – practically *tête-à-tête*.

So next day, today, Janet was taken away from them all. Janet was not accustomed to being followed about; today, the whole of Theodora's attention weighted her movements. She was investigated; her unmarried friend showed a lucid perplexity. Perhaps it did seem odd how one filled one's days.

But: 'I must just ask So-and-so . . .' she went on. 'I must just see about the such-and-such.'

'Oh! Do you really *have* to?'

And Theodora, in ironic patience, ground out cigarette after cigarette against the range, the churn, the mangle, against so many doors of 'offices' that were meanwhile – it must be owned without apparent reference to Janet – calmly functioning. 'I don't see *how* one "sees after" or "sees about," ' remarked Theodora. 'Either one does a thing oneself or one doesn't do it. Do explain, Janet.' In the dairy she ate a spoonful of cream, tasted the butter, felt sick but refused to go away. In the steam of the laundry she glowered like a djinn. 'My beautiful,' she observed finally, 'how you do fuss, don't you?' Janet tried to remember if Theodora had really been like this last time. and to understand how, if so, she came to be here again.

As they crossed the bleach-green a bell swung high up in the stable cupola, knocking sparks from the blue air. One or two pigeons wheeled. 'Twelve o'clock,' said Janet.

'So what do you do *now*?'

Janet not quite innocently said she had letters to write. They went into the library where Janet looked through a file, pressed her blotter open, took her cheque-book out of a locked drawer – she fell in in every way with her bank's ideas. Theodora paced round the library, clicking her cigarette-case. Janet turned her dark head sideways in concentration; there was so much to think of, to do; she was in arrears. 'There they go –' she sighed involuntarily, as Lady Elfrida and Considine passed the window. *Their* holiday was not at an end. Had she, in their company for these first bright days of summer – her first, perhaps, visible summer; when the season had halted for her, smiling at her direct – too entirely disengaged herself? She herself still lived and had to command emotion: they seemed to have died young. She lived –

74

look at all these letters: she unscrewed the top of her fountain-pen.
'There they go,' sighed Janet.

'There go who?' said Theodora jealously.

'Elfrida and Considine.'

'Oh!... Shall you ever finish those letters?'

'Dear Theodora, I cannot write if you loom,' said Janet mildly.

'Darling, I cannot believe you can write at all. Look at the letters you send me.'

The library certainly had become oppressive. Janet was supposed by them all to have no nerves; she agreed, with hardly a glance at herself. She wished Theodora embroidered, or even ever sat down. She supposed, Theodora is bored, Theodora is fond of me. It was twelve o'clock now; at twenty to one she would cross to the sofa, sit idle lest Theodora should be offended, give her entire attention, say: 'Well, Theodora...?'

Then she would listen to Theodora till a quarter past one, when the children must come in to wash for lunch: they ignored the Swiss maid's peahen screaming: Janet must go out to add a note of authority. (Note: did Anna make Hermione disobedient?) Meanwhile, if a blue-bottle came into the library she must not attend – why did one not put wire gauze over windows like the Americans? – and if anyone came to the door she would frown. She would listen. Something was always the matter with Theodora – something was generally the matter with Edward.... She fulfilled her engagement: 'Well, Theodora...?' she said, closing her blotter.

But Theodora was going to be sarcastic. She could not pass fatuity and said something about the children's hour. But Janet amiably sat there and looked at her hands. This was her sort of friendliness, simply a disposition.

'How long are *they* here for?' asked Theodora, ominously staring across the lawn.

'Are who?'

'Your couple.'

But if Theodora were not like this, she would not be like anything. 'Oh, indefinitely, I hope,' said Janet. 'I've no idea.'

'And what does poor Edward say?'

'I have no idea.'

'You'd rather not have,' stated Theodora accurately. 'Well, I daresay it's time *something* happened.'

'But, Theodora, so many things happen to you.'

This Theodora quite overruled. 'I suppose it has all been delightful these last few days? How bold you have been, Janet!'

'We're so fond of them both. I don't see why we can't be natural.'

'That seems a rather curious observation from *you*,' said Theodora heavily.

'Does it?... Tell me about the Tyrol.'

'Good God, I didn't come here to tell you about the Tyrol. Have you been happy?'

'Yes, very, thank you,' said Janet. Sitting here with her back to the window she found the green glare of the lawn reflected along the walls, the glazed bookcase, the flank of the tallboise. These all had an immaterial quality as in firelight but drawn up in a stillness like water's did not waver. She felt, through the open window, summer come into the cool room and touch her shoulders. 'It's been very fine,' she added.

Theodora slid from the end of the sofa and bumped herself into comfort among the cushions. She heard steps turn back in the hall; she knew they must all know Janet was 'coping' with Theodora, who would not be here long.

'The fact is,' she exclaimed, 'Lady Elfrida's a fool. She longs to snub me. She tried at both the weddings and several times since. She laughs before I have finished speaking and says: "Oh, no, do you really?" The fact is, she can't bear other people to be amusing – well, look at poor dear Considine, look at you! She does love her own little angle. She's really the worst kind of woman – no, listen, darling – quite automatic –'

Janet thought back through this slowly. 'But she likes Lewis; surely he is amusing?'

'No,' said his sister's friend.

'And I think Hermione's funny, don't you? She likes Hermione.'

'Anyhow, *I'm* Hermione's godmother.'

'Of course,' agreed Janet, alarmed by the pounce in her friend's manner. 'Hermione adores you,' she added.

'Much good may that do her,' said Theodora darkly. 'And does she adore Edward?'

For Edward was Hermione's godfather. This had been Rodney's idea – and most, Theodora thought, most indelicate. She eyed Janet's profile. They had intended, of course, to have asked Lewis. But Lewis was 'so many godfathers' – Rodney had suddenly made this other gesture. Lewis had told Marise who told Theodora that Edward and Laurel had been, at the time, much discomposed by the suggestion and did not know how to reply. Continually, they were being worried by this sort of thing; pheasants, flowers from Batts, an invitation for Laurel to winter with Janet abroad. Stupefaction had, on that early occasion, carried the day with Edward. Now on Sundays, birthdays, family festivals his goddaughter tilted her gilt reflection about inside a silver mug of ironic magnificence, two-handled like the trophy that indeed it was. This celestial tie with their father gave Hermione what was, in view of the general Tilney sense of Meggatt delinquency, her sole moral advantage over Anna and Simon.

'And of course,' went on Theodora, 'Lady Elfrida does bore me. She's the most tiresome kind of *cathédrale engloutie*, full of backwashes and large drowned bells.'

'Nonsense,' said Janet kindly, hoping it pleased Theodora to be so clever.

'And I also observe –'

The fact was, Theodora could not keep off that extinct sin. Her resentment appeared surprising. But that old crater, now so cheerfully verdant, accounted, she thought, for the persistence of an emotional Edward in Janet's landscape. Though the whole theory of victimization was disagreeable to Theodora, she could have forgiven Edward a childish anguish if this had not perpetuated itself. She could not forgive him this tenure it gave him, this mortmain on Janet's spirit.

Theodora was profoundly mistaken. Janet did not find Edward pathetic – or if she found him pathetic she was unmoved. Her ruling was largely domestic; she was impatient for order, distinguished grief from grievance, and deplored grievance as a delay of the faculties. Janet's refusal to see Edward's bruises had been definitive. For the root Edward had in her consciousness, a sort of vital misgiving one had only to love Janet to have suspected, Theodora might well have looked back to her own first view of him: a young man, a bridegroom, isolated by an occasion, stepping out through a window. She might have marked that wedding-day for the fatal climax of his hesitations, a misdirected lover's. Had there been somewhere, sometime, a moment when Laurel's sister took Edward's measure; some glance of hers away from him to perfection of which he could not but be aware; from which glance, from which moment they both lived on involuntarily? There had been no question: unasked, the question always was at her elbow. With that unasked question, unanswerable, Edward need have no concern – but concern racked him. Just once they quarrelled, that hot night in London: now it would not be possible to violate Janet's incuriosity.

But the silent question was at her elbow still. Urgent, like Hermione (who wisely, when she did not want to be sent away, hardly breathed, hardly made herself known, made no claims). Like Hermione, always too much with her mother, too tensely present, it interposed, distracting her, made other intimacy impossible. At all times it was impossible to be alone with Janet.

The clock-hand moved to a quarter past. The pair of cheerful shadows, crossing the lawn again, crossed the wall, the bookcases ... There were moments – Edward's handwriting on an envelope, his name casually in Janet's talk – when Theodora, exasperated, sighted a large possibility of destruction; when Janet's composure became something precariously but calmly held, some very delicate glass or a dish piled high with fruit that balanced curve on curve just not tottering. To splinter the vase, to knock the dish out of Janet's hand, Theodora had only to cry: 'You still love him.'

A wild enough kind of justice. But violence was not distasteful to Theodora. If Batts found her a trifle over-emphatic, they could have no idea that she had once kicked through a door-panel, and once, annoyed on Leman, upset a canoe and made someone swim for it. Janet, who did not regard Theodora as dangerous, feared by the end of their talk that her friend had still to unbosom herself. Brushing Theodora's ash off the cretonne she said: 'The rest will be out for tea. You must tell me about Marise.'

'Will Rodney be there?'

'I'm sure Rodney would like to hear about Marise too,' said Janet.

5

Tilney hair grew quickly, high off the forehead, low at the nape: even Simon had it. Long before Hermione Meggatt was due at the hairdresser's Simon's appearance became 'artistic' (a drooping forelock), quite at odds with his character. While the 'bob' framing Anna's expression declined from a cool young page's to a comedian's, turning out at the ends. It was Theodora who pointed out, almost upon arrival, how fast deterioration set in with the young Tilneys. Their grandmother, seeing the pair for the first time at a disadvantage, rallied to them surprisingly. After an unsuccessful attempt with her nail-scissors she offered to take the two children herself to the hairdresser at Market Keaton. She thought: after all, we Tilneys do stand together. One afternoon, therefore, Considine packed the impassive children into the back of his car, where their bare knees, parted, grilled on the hot cushions. Lady Elfrida, tilting her hat-brim over her face, for she feared the sun, took her place in front. Considine was to drive them.

Janet had not been sensitive on the Tilneys' behalf. But she was glad to see their grandmother's wings out over them, even a little. 'Grandmother's kind,' she said, leaning into the car to give Anna her gloves; then, going up the steps again, remained dark in the doorway to watch the departure. Hermione, who was overexcited, was not to accompany them. *She* did not care, she said. Lady Elfrida had the list of Janet's messages safe in her handbag – no, oh dear, in the other handbag, what a good thing one had looked! Hermione was sent flying upstairs three times for this, for that, then for Anna's grandmother's parasol. But it was a good thing to start so calmly.

It was certainly hot. Lady Elfrida viewed the dark-green scene with regret as they slipped off under the beeches. At such an hour, similes were postprandial; like gooseberry fool the silence closed in behind them; their speed soon jumbled the brightness of afternoon, turning it like a salad . . . But she had the town-dweller's love of going to town: Considine beside her was all complaisance, a panama and a chin. He could digest anywhere. Hedges crisp with budding wild roses, banks in a high foam of cow-parsley soon gave way to allotments. Hoardings rushed up eager for their attention; scarlet and yellow petrol pumps, like a civic procession, marched out to meet them more than a mile from the town.

'Market Keaton's "developing",' Considine said, regretful.

'It's changed,' said Lady Elfrida. For the place had scandalous associations.

They had misgivings: would the hairdresser be awake? Here the town hall clock struck three to an empty square, inattentive, pitted with pole-sockets: not a stall up yet for tomorrow's market. A cat's yawn gave the note of the afternoon. Pavements sleepily glared; over the butcher's a piano played in its sleep. All down the streets the lettered awnings were low, and women, girls for the day in brief cotton dresses, crossed from shadow to shadow. The town did not know itself; it became a seaside town high and dry; in contradiction to nature some bright shadow, some idea of unreal pleasure trailed over it. Bow-fronted houses bulged here and there from the flat stucco; in shadow, the Gothic bank was cut out in slate on the glare; opposite, the brick 'Plough' flushed in a bacchic dream.

The hairdresser must be awake; they had telephoned.

Considine had promised Anna an ice; the car slipped in low gear along the kerb; she prospected sideways. She could not say much for the town's amenities: too many hardware shops full of zinc and fibre, buckets stacked painfully tight, carpet brushes dangling without invitation. Was life necessitous? She was glad when a lady stopped to buy two geraniums; she looked back; the pots were being wrapped up in blue paper; the lady and the florist yawned. The confectioners were meanly appointed: yes, there would be cornflour in the ices. Never the time and the place . . . For she passed Rumpelmayer's so often, but with her father always, on the way to the London Museum.

Whereas to Simon the town seemed to sell only hats, thin-coloured ribbon, overmantles. His friend the A.A. man was not on point duty. The chemist's window had baby foods in a pyramid, no cameras. There would have been no harm in *showing* Considine a camera like you wanted, in the chemist's window.

But everyone knew who they were. Some fine brick houses fronted the High Street; Anna could be quite certain she saw the curtains twitch. Petunia was the colour of their grandmother's hat; also, at one time she had been very much in the papers. The gratified hairdresser was at his door; the Tilneys, multiplied by

importance, all got out of the car. In the hot vibration going up
from the bonnet dogs were like minnows, doors moved like reeds
under water and ladies swam. Considine shut off the engine and,
arms folded, immediately dropped asleep in nodding confidence
with his knees. Hot? Not as Considine knew it. To Anna, up at
the window of the ladies' saloon being buttoned into a starched
cape, he looked down there, foreshortened, like a daddy-long-legs
rather than a spider. Though she had his bad character on the
best authority.

Lady Elfrida could see at once that the hairdresser was going
to be stupid. 'Cut it like a bell,' she said distinctly, 'only not at
the ends – more like a mushroom. *Not* like the Knave of Hearts,
that would look dreadful, wouldn't it? You do see, don't you? –
Wait, give me a pencil –'

Meanwhile, the hairdresser took off a safe inch along Anna's
fringe.

'I don't think Mother would like me to have all this off my
fringe,' said Anna when he had finished.

'Oh dear,' exclaimed Lady Elfrida, who had been reading the
tariff. 'It does make you look like a pony.' She said to the hairdresser in the friendliest way, 'I see you permanent wave?'

'Certainly, my lady –'

'Oh no, thank you – I just wanted a pencil.'

'Mother likes it *en Jeanne d'Arc*,' said Anna presently.

'Oh, I shouldn't mind about that in the country; I should
just have it nice and neat. Do you really give face massage, Mr
Hesketh?'

She had been going to add: 'I didn't know people round here
had faces.' Certainly what she hoped to meet when she looked
over a gate or went to a door would be something ruddy and
various, not to pattern, a free surface for pleasure – more of a
'countenance'. But now she went anxiously to the top of the
stairs. 'I hope,' she said, 'they are not putting anything on the
little boy's hair down below?'

But it was too late, already in the gentlemen's saloon they had
anointed Simon with violet oil. Lady Elfrida quite lost her nerve
and said they must all go as soon as possible, to the grocer's. 'Just
finish the best way you can,' she said, eyeing, beyond disparagement, Anna's reflection. 'So long as it's all the same length it
looks quite nice.'

'I think I look worse than I did,' said Anna gloomily.

'Oh no, lovely. Now come and we'll choose the fish.'

'I think Uncle Considine wants me to have an ice.'

'Oh no, Anna darling, because we've got to go to the chemist's. And Uncle Rodney wants all that wire-netting ordered – Some other day.'

'But some other day I might be having some other ice.'

Considering that the child's appearance was ruined she did seem at least to be owed this. What Theodora was certain to say would be most uncalled for: Theodora herself had been a hideous little girl. Nowadays, though her figure was nice, something must be the matter. She pounced: it was curious – could *she* have wanted to marry Edward? She had been quite disqualified by that blue hat. Besides, she was then fifteen – and had they not met the first time at his own wedding? So it could not have been that. Besides, she had passions for women – awkward, such a tax on behaviour, like nausea at meals. Or was this perhaps for effect, did she mean to be funny like that? Because she made Elfrida feel quite hysterical. Surely people were odder, or was it just that one met them? Had these years, with their still recent sense of catastrophe, brought out curious people, like toads after rain? Perhaps she was anxious to please – but could that be cause for anxiety?

Lady Elfrida made her way distractedly to the car.

'Oh, Anna's *ice*, Considine.' By reflex action he put out a half-crown. 'Can you smell poor Simon? Someone will have to wash him. He'd better have an ice too.'

'We wouldn't like to go in alone,' said Anna modestly.

It would have been better for Considine if Edward himself, in the first place, had never been born; all the same, tipping back his hat from his face he got out of the car with docility and smiled at the Tilneys. Watching, aware of his charm, she had once more to account for that stupefying cessation of love, positive as the passion itself and like a flood not arrestable, coming down on them both when they were both entirely for each other at last, in Paris. That inquiry, that just perceptible pause of his, face to face with her, when he had gone for less than a moment into abeyance – she had let that less than moment eternalize itself and harden till, though so fine, it could be driven down through living heart and body without swerving. His metamorphosis? She had no place for the living dog: there could have been honey in the mouth of the dead lion.

'The car?' Anna prompted. (For they might well be arrested.)

'I park anywhere,' said Considine. The three went into the teashop. In the inside, full of sun, marble tables looked warm to the touch; in the window flies thrust their long proboscises through muslin swathing the pastries and loitered, wistful, over the glass bells.

'I shall go to the grocer's, then to the chemist's,' Elfrida called after them. 'Then you bring the car along and pay, if we find we must.'

The grocer's went off triumphantly; Janet's clear writing caused her no hesitation. (When she shopped from her cook's list at Harrod's she was continually humiliated.) She bought a blue crock of ginger on her own account, for Hermione, cheerfully dropped her gloves in the sawdust, thanked everybody and was much reassured. A dear cat fawned on her parasol, sorry to see her go.

But at the chemist's, a dark shop like the inside of a camera, she immediately felt apprehensive and wished she had not come into town at all. As the chemist came round a weighing-machine with a particular air of importance she nearly said: 'Don't –' But she could avert nothing: there was a message. Mrs Meggatt had telephoned. 'Oh?' said Lady Elfrida. His manner, the antiseptics, the assistant's ferret-like bundling behind the counter, the Kodak lady, *démodée* in stripes in a perpetual high wind, had unnerved her before he could speak again.

Mrs Meggatt would be glad if Lady Elfrida Tilney would telephone to her as soon as possible. The chemist offered his telephone and, in advance, his solicitude. With a strong sense of being attracted to something fatal, she squeezed in behind the bottles. The chemist's assistant stopped bundling, she heard a voice in the street; then, in the street, in the shop, between the houses, the hot urban silence disintegrated in motes under her anxiety, like indoor air with sun suddenly upon it.

Janet must have been waiting: she came at once.

'Edward has come; he is here. He wants to take the children back to town with him at once, this afternoon. Can you all come back as soon as possible? Perhaps you had better tell them.'

'Whatever's the matter?'

'I don't really know.'

'Is he – is it being tiresome, Janet?'

'Yes.'

'I am telephoning from the chemist's.'

'I know,' said Janet, and rang off.

There should have been more. Was this one of her silences, an aversion of her look from yours, too eloquent; or had Edward come in? Returning to the counter, Lady Elfrida delivered her orders from Janet's list. 'We will call back for the parcels,' she said. But they never did.

The ices, bright pink, tasting of their colour, were clapped between wafers. Anna with numbing stomach was well into her third; she knew that this must be pleasure. Her face of angelic insensibility tilted over her saucer. Simon took large bites out of a macaroon, then quickly sucked up raspberryade through two straws and let them go down together. Considine had asked Anna to eat his ices for him; he sat, feet apart, on the iron feet of the table, thinking what little beggars they were. Elfrida had placed no restrictions upon his hospitality and he saw no reason why the children should not be allowed to kill themselves. He almost regretted no satisfaction of his own could be so agreeably fatal.

Simon paused. 'There are two currants squashed on your elbow,' he said to Considine. Someone at the table before them had eaten Banbury cakes.

'They stain,' said Anna quietly, as he picked them off. 'Uncle Considine, how many ices would *you* be eating?'

'Six,' said Considine promptly.

'Oh, I don't think I could quite...'

'Grandmother would be furious,' said Simon tranquilly, stretching out for another cake.

His sister answered: 'Not if it's not her fault.'

Considine liked acuteness in women. 'That's no way to talk!' he said provocatively, and Anna, who had resented till now a certain lack of social surface, rallied to her sex. Leaning towards him, glancing from her hand to his chin, she said in confidence: 'Hermione's always being sick; have you noticed?'

'Your father was always being sick,' said Considine, idly reminiscent.

'He was unhappy,' she said with some pride.

'Indeed.'

'He had no real home – Simon, I don't think you ought to take a new cake till you've finished swallowing.'

'Swallowing yourself,' said Simon excusably.

'Oo, *tu quoque*! – I'm afraid there's another currant on your sleeve now, Uncle Considine. Your poor suit! – Were you fond of our father?'

Considine looked round for the waitress. 'Another ice!'

'But you are fond of children, aren't you? You gave him a bear.'

Simon, hastily swallowing, said: 'Did you ever give him a camera?'

'Didn't you give him a bear?'

'I expect,' said Simon, 'he *was* pleased. Like I should be if anyone gave me a camera.'

'Oh, he liked the bear, did he?' said Considine. 'You never know.' In fact, now he came to remember, Elfrida had never mentioned the bear since its mobled entry that night before Christmas. He had just heard, in some other connection, that Edward had been taken to bed in hysterics.

'He never liked animals much,' said Anna thoughtfully. 'That bear was sent back here when Grandmother went to live in Paris. It's got all moth-eaten now; doesn't that seem a pity?'

'How do *you* know?' asked Considine rashly.

'Hermione told me. She showed me the bear.'

Simon sat bending one of the straws round his thumb. 'I expect any present is nice.' he said wistfully.

Simon was awful about hints, no one could either trace or suppress this terribly common trait: he was nearly always successful. Anna disowned him. Patting her shorn fringe she said socially: 'Doesn't it sometimes seem queer Hermione and I should be first cousins?'

'No,' said Considine forcibly.

'Oh, *I* think so. You see, I'm so lucky; I don't get excited and I'm never sick. I think we have quite different characters . . .'

But she was nowhere – Considine had radiantly turned to the door.

Elfrida had come in. Down the long shop, narrow and cumbered like the past, with its dull mirrors, she came very tall, *distraite*, balancing nervously in her speed like a ship just launched.

Her bright hat focused the sunlight; she disturbed the stale enclosed afternoon that like a cake under glass night after night had covered without renewing. She approached blankly, as though to await rather than to join them; and this unawareness, old in a thousand of her approaches, lending the ultimate meeting and greeting the whole charm of fortuity, was for the thousand-and-first time new to him. She called out the stranger in him to meet her; the children saw him accessible, hopeful, struck.

'So here you are,' he said, rising.

'Now we've all got to go home at once,' cried Lady Elfrida. 'Come, Anna, come along, Simon: it's such fun, your father is here.'

'Where?'

'Batts.'

'But he's in London.'

Reaching round for their hats and jerseys, pulling anxiously at their chairs, she explained their good fortune. '*Edward?*' said Considine, blank. She frowned on his incredulity; the preposterous had become her element. 'Oh Simon, *come!*' she cried. 'All right, bring that cake along with you. You're both going back to London.'

'How do you know?' said Anna suspiciously.

'Don't ask silly questions.'

It became clear to the children, *someone* was in the wrong.

'Now?' said Simon.

'Why?' said Anna.

'For a surprise – won't that be fun!'

'No,' said Simon, while Anna objected. 'We've just settled down here.' No doubt this was a prank, and going up in the train their father would wish them to play American bandits. One would have preferred a father more like Mr Darling, less like Peter Pan. Anna, who had re-read and was familiar with all her mother's books on child management, could have told them that this was bad for children, being rushed about in the heat. Enough to bring one out in a rash, stop one's inside or give one a complex.

'My clothes are all at the wash,' she said, getting up with dignity.

'I wonder you aren't excited,' exclaimed her grandmother. 'Uncle Considine and I would love to be going to London as a surprise.'

'Then why don't you go?' said Anna coldly.

'Oh, *don't be annoying*, Anna!' Children were certainly at a discount. With their hats at curious angles, with some publicity she hurried them to the car. Anna hoped someone noticed how well they took it. While Elfrida reflected: at all events, one had the situation well in hand. 'Children take anything naturally if one is calm with them,' she said·to Considine. The children's present appearance might well be a shock, a salutary shock, to Edward. And it would be for Laurel to disinfect Simon. How he would reek in the hot train, poor little boy.

Considine was not a support. 'Well, it seems to me odd,' he kept saying placidly, and 'Elfrida, do be calm with that child; she is full of ices.' He walked round the car, kicked each tyre, looked into the engine, and remained apparently doubled in speculation above the self-starter. He supposed, some resurgence of 'fuss', a hardy perennial. Well, Edward was fortunate; few young men had time for their feelings. So much for Whitehall . . . And yet one was always hearing, 'Poor Edward is so overworked, so rushed . . .' Moral hyperaesthesia. 'Thank God he was not *my* son: I was in Egypt.'

'We shall want more petrol,' remarked Considine to Elfrida.

'Really, you can be annoying!'

'My dear, it won't further anything if we run out.'

'Perhaps our mother is dying,' thought Anna, in the back of the car.

'The parcels?'

'No – no – no – Yes, better call for the fish.'

As they turned in at the gates Lady Elfrida saw Edward ahead of them, walking hurriedly, nervously, on the avenue in a dark suit, straight from town. She made a movement to Considine – wishing perhaps to stop the car. But at the sound of the car, Edward took a line off through the trees, without waving.

6

'I know,' said Janet, and hung up the receiver. She could say nothing more, facts were not in order. Also, Edward came in from the terrace. The position of the telephone here was characteristic: it was for barest communication only, and in the hall.

. Edward did not surprise her; she had heard him halt on the gravel; before that twice he had passed a window. He had gone out for a turn, he said; to pace out the interim. As he came up the steps she had him exposed a moment in full sunshine before in irresolute outline he darkened the doorway.

Janet said composedly: 'Your mother. She's bringing the children straight back.'

'Is she? Thank you, Janet . . . It's hot out there.'

'I should think so. But I'm afraid I can't get them packed in time for the five-thirty-six. Will the seven-five do?'

'I suppose she thinks I am mad?' said Edward suddenly, glancing at the telephone.

'– As it is, some of their things will have to be sent after them. Hermione's maid is out for the afternoon. Shall I write this to Laurel – she may wonder – or shall you remember to tell her?'

Laurel never expected Edward to control agitation; much had been based on a strong feeling she had for spontaneity. So that he was surprised by the tone of decided reproof in which Janet added: 'I can't think why you should go out without your hat.'

Had he suffered? He passed his hand over the top of his head.

She said: 'Well, shall we come into the library?' She was so patient, he must be an invalid; so without concern for him, he must be sick from some over-indulgence. As a domestic emergency, he came under control.

'Won't Theodora –?'

'No, I sent her out to find Rodney.'

'Because I suppose,' said Edward, looking with horror at the library door, 'we had better talk.'

'I suppose so.'

'Or could we walk somewhere – down to those trees?'

'I should stay still while you can, Edward; you've had a tiring day.'

So he followed her and, with an air of fatality, closed the library door. Standing beside the high mantelpiece she kept her barely ironic formal manner; this was to be an interview. Thus, as a girl, she had enraged him in Trevor Square. Now, more kindly, established, his hostess, she disclaimed her advantage.

For from the terrace he had viewed the whole mass of her trees, at this season in their magnificence; thoughtless great plants vitally embracing the daylight, exercising upon his distraction a physical dominance. He saw the contours of the land in their whole mild power. She possessed the skyline; the sky, the large afternoon were bounded by her and localized. And narrowly pacing her terrace he had measured the whole of his own territory, the barren and pitted territory of emotion.

'I'm sorry,' he said, 'to come down like this and disturb you – and everything.'

'I suppose you felt you must.'

'But whatever did you expect?'

Though she still did not look his way her repose had an absolute candour. 'We hoped by now you might let.things pass. We've respected your – your feeling for quite a.long time, Edward.'

'Yes, I know you . . .'

'Yes?' She too willingly paused, and there ensued a contest of silences, during which she did not sir.

Till he exclaimed: 'But why *now*? What has changed? Why, *now* should I be less what you all call impossible? Why have my mother here with Considine *now*, out of all these years, with Anna and Simon here?'

'It seemed the one thing to do,' said Janet. 'It was so fine,' she added, and after some seconds' reflection produced no amendment.

'Does nothing seem to you difficult?'

'I don't know. This seemed natural.'

Her unnatural sense of the natural . . . She remained a dark stranger, too near him. While she assumed – as then in her awkward girlhood – some understanding between them, speechless, fatal without love.

'But do things like that change?' said Edward who, as she would not look at him, would not look at her, but fixed closely the object at which she too was looking, the pediment of a candlestick.

'We are all so much older; by now our children are people. Surely we must have arrived –' This became too difficult for her thought, she abandoned it and continued: 'I suppose we gave you the benefit of the doubt. We all take up so much more room in this house, or something. Of course, it's unlucky that Rodney should be Considine's nephew, but no more so than that you should be Elfrida's son. I do feel it's time we thought about something else. It's unhealthy, surely, don't you think. Like having to stay indoors with the blinds down because of a funeral always going by.'

'Which has been, naturally, always my fault,' said Edward stonily.

'Not quite,' she said simply. 'But one has got to be practical. You know this house is not large; our friends like to come here, in summer specially; we like to have them; that is our idea of a home. The summers are really too short, if our friends must not meet. We cannot keep asking Considine to leave here, his own house, and go to his club when he is so little in England anyhow. We cannot expect your mother to stay in London without a cook because she once ruined herself – Yes, I did mean ruined herself; isn't that how you've made her see it? – For that matter, we could not refuse Theodora when her flat was let and it rained so much in Austria, though she does bore your mother and bully Considine. Your mother and Considine amuse each other; I've never made friends much; I never knew two people, except sisters, could be so happy. If you do think it shocking for your children to see two people amusing each other who once made each other wretched, of course you are quite right to take them away. Only this, Edward: I don't know how much Anna and Simon do know, but when they must hear what happened, surely this, what they see here now, would be nice for them to remember? Otherwise, I don't see how you can bear them to grow up.'

'I suppose I hardly can,' said Edward involuntarily.

'Oh Edward, don't be ridiculous! Then why were they ever born?'

'But their world –'

'But after all, there only *is* one world; and that's naturally awkward sometimes, like sharing a room.'

'You talk of amusement – but they were utterly through with each other. You know, we all know; it was wretched: they couldn't even marry.'

'Well, they are amused: perhaps you and I couldn't understand how. They are the same age, they have the same angle, they are comfortable together; I daresay we all seem a shade absurd to them. I wouldn't mind that, would you? At most times they must have to keep so much to themselves. They are surprised at the same things. They talk . . .'

'They had nothing more left to say.'

'Perhaps not then.'

'When they were in love?' he cried, incredulous.

'I can't tell,' said Janet. 'I never have much to say. Have I?'

'I can't tell – you've never talked to me.'

'Oh, I don't think this does much good,' exclaimed Janet. 'Do you want me to go on?' She moved the candlestick, then its fellow, a little nearer to the clock. Edward walked away from her down the library, drew up and stared at some shelves. 'No, go on,' he said.

'They talk about ... what became of their friends, their investments, what he has done, what she would have liked to do, what they both don't like. And spas and places, and marriages –'

'Marriage?'

'No, whom people married.'

'How do you know?'

'I've heard them.'

'And why should this be specially good for the children?'

'– I do hope, Edward, we shan't quarrel again – Because they're *your* children!'

He committed her fully to this, underlining the remark by a complete silence. She had to turn round: he replaced a book. Nothing further had to be understood; they let the remark remain between them, a sheer awkwardness. 'Edward –' she began; this was the first break in her manner; despair came through, so personal, so positive that it was like the carrying-in of a light in which the whole subject wavered a moment, to become smaller and plainer. 'This does no good,' said Janet.

Silence took this again on its surface, a glass wall against which she stood excluded. She stood powerless, looking through at her life, at, not regainable, her whole habit of mind. This, like a house long inhabited without feeling and vacated easily, bore in, re-visited in its emptiness, an anguishing sense of her no-presence even in the past. 'I am here,' she thought, and pressed the mantelpiece which again in a few months would redden over the firelight. But the marble contact lessened under her hand; either the stone warmed or her hand, chilling, became insensible of coldness. Even the room, this high sober library, green with outdoor reflections, was now empty of Janet and Edward, as though both had turned and gone out by different doors, or had never come in.

He looked round, possibly to speak. But – 'Edward,' she suddenly asked, 'what brought you down here *today*? I mean, why today? They've been here a week; it's more than a week since I told Laurel.'

'Of course: I remember your letter.'

'We were beginning to hope you mightn't mind,' she said naïvely.

'Were you?' said Edward, curious. 'I don't know if I did mind. I was just entirely taken aback. I suppose I had thought things were understood. But of course if you could do that, I couldn't do anything. I just let things be. My dear, if you are working nine hours a day nothing is a catastrophe – Oh, I daresay nothing *is* a catastrophe – Outside work, I haven't thought of anything for a week. I've got back to dinner and walked round the Gardens and gone to bed. We've got a beastly little dog now and I take it out. I supposed I must never have trusted you, so it didn't matter.'

'Yes, I see,' said Janet. 'Then why did it matter today?'

'We got a letter.'

'I don't see . . .'

'Laurel got a letter from Theodora.'

'I didn't know they wrote to each other.'

'They don't.'

'Then what had she to say?'

'I can't tell you,' he said sharply.

Janet had had no idea that letters of this kind left her house. She thought: 'What a pity . . . How horrid.' Aloud she said: 'I think you'd better tell me, if it really worries you. But I shouldn't take much notice. Theodora is odd; I suppose it's her sense of humour.'

'You don't understand.'

'Well, no, naturally. Show me the letter.'

'No, I couldn't,' said Edward, appalled. 'That would be absolutely impossible!'

'Nonsense,' said Janet, and held out her hand impatiently.

'Very well,' said Edward. His voice went up to a cold high note of indifference; he was no longer concerned with her peace of mind. He looked through his pocket-book and passed her some folded sheets of the blue familiar Batts notepaper. 'Here you are,' said Edward. It did not matter to him if the house fell.

Theodora had written:

'. . . pleasant, though I am so bored. The days are wobbly and hot, we go up and down to the vicarage. Once we've been out to tennis. The nights, though, are perfect *fêtes galantes* – for all the rest. The window sills don't cool all night. I sit outside the library – no one for *me* to stroll with – the children sit out above. They go through their collection of glow-worms and talk about their grandmother – you have no idea! I forget, is Anna a little girl who has been Told, or Not been told? Not, I should think, or she'd hardly be so ingenuous. I think, below, how boringly one really does sin – Though of course, dear Laurel, how should I know? Don't snub Anna, she's wonderful. Besides, she is bound to grow up to a disappointment. Meanwhile, the lawn is like a hot promenade in August; people keep passing and smiling. Rodney and Janet pick up more glow-worms for the children's collection. It's like Rodney and Janet, who can't love reciprocally, to have *this* here for a spectacle.'

And further on:

'Innsbrück itself could not be duller. No doubt it's my fault; I snubbed their last young man. Besides, I asked myself. They were all getting on so nicely – I must say, they are still. So I sit writing letters – even to you, dear Laurel – I could wish you were both here, but I'm afraid you'd find *that* impossible. I'm afraid it will rain by July; you will all sit indoors at nights and only half know Batts, which is so full of possibilities. But perhaps you may like that better. And Janet must be the perfect sister. Do stop her fussing about the dairy; there is always quite enough butter; I don't know what more she wants. I brush her hair at nights; I brush well. Never let her cut it.'

Janet read, at all times, with an annoying slowness. Now, with an utter lack of expression, she re-read the letter. 'But I can't think,' she said at last, 'why Laurel bothered to show you this.' And later: 'But there's nothing here at all true that I didn't know.'

But on Edward the letter's appearance, or the very fact of her reading, had renewed the letter's whole agonizing effect. Janet's very impassivity seemed to conduct pain to him.

'But you know,' she said, 'that I know Theodora is rather – I suppose really rather a bounder. I can't think why; the Thirdmans are so nice.'

'That's not the immediate point . . .'

'Yes, it is the point. I'd no idea she was so bored.'

'Oh, she's jealous, obviously – Why do you let her brush your hair?'

'Do you mind?' said Janet, and intent once more on the

93

mantelpiece once more moved the candlesticks away from the clock.

'I seem to mind everything, don't I?' said Edward bitterly. 'How impossible I must be.'

'Not just impossible; jealous.'

'Of whom?' he said quickly.

'Your mother; she seems to have such a lovely time. Perhaps we all are.'

'Speak for yourself, Janet.'

'I do, always. But *you* can't bear anything to be going on that you're not in. You behave like someone who's missed a train. You really do, Edward.'

'I can't help what happened to me.'

'Nothing ever has happened to *you*.'

'Do you mind?'

'I suppose so.' She still had the letter; she looked from the letter into the fireplace, but there was nothing but cold, stacked logs. So more or less absently and without ostentation she tore and retore the letter across. There hung heavily, then dissolved in the air between them, the fumes of a potent vulgarity. 'All this comes to is this: the children – I daresay Hermione as much as Anna – have been making guesses about what went wrong with your mother. I suppose they've heard gossip; I think, if so, they ought to be told. It is hot, so after dinner we walk about out of doors, which is boring for Theodora, because she is odd man out – it is not our fault that she won't join us. And, of course, we smile, which is more than Theodora or you seem able to bear. She thinks Rodney's and my marriage dull; I daresay most marriages do look like that. And she did want to get a rise out of you and Laurel. I cannot think why you should both be such idiots as to play into her hands . . .'

'. . . What about the "spectacle"?'

'You know that's untrue; we can't deal with that,' she said coldly.

'But you can't like it.'

She said: 'I don't think it's worth discussing. As it regards me and Rodney, I think it is something you, Edward, might leave alone. The letter's torn up.'

Edward, standing closer to her than they were both aware, saw her hands tighten on the mantelpiece. 'It's wretched,' he said, 'that you both were ever brought in in this context at all – As you say, that's Theodora's manner: I think you're mistaken in having her here at all – But because this affects you and you can't be asked to be clear, it's unfair to accuse me of distortion. All delicacy is on your side; you can see I can't speak at all without outraging something: you don't let a thing pass. I am utterly humiliated by everything you make me say. Nothing I say is myself. I loathe this whole business!' said Edward passionately.

'You brought yourself here; you need never have come.'

'I had to see you,' said Edward shortly.

'You wanted to show me that letter.'

The cold, mounting excitement under her manner communicated itself to Edward and, like fever, effected a disembodiment. So that his thought, detaching itself from the self in anguish, ranged with delirious boldness; hardly thought at all, detached from feeling. And as when in fever the freed, weightless thought going down street after street or penetrating a forest, halts, finds one house or one tree and fuses with this utterly, becoming the house or tree past hope of escape, Edward's thought stopped and flared at a point where dread and desire ran round the circle to meet. He was Janet. 'If you and I had fallen in love – But I didn't want that,' he said clearly. He had less than a moment to take up her first full look that passed his almost in flight as she turned to the door.

7

'This is very nice,' said Rodney, coming in cheerfully to greet Edward.

He had, of course, a shrewd idea this was not very nice. Theodora, pursued hot-foot by Hermione, had hurried across the fields to tell him that Edward had just arrived, without warning, furious, in a fly, without a suitcase, to take away his children who were being corrupted. A spontaneity in Theodora's enjoyment of the crisis made her almost lovable; she frankly glowed. While Hermione, dancing, was naturally in her element.

'Have you any idea –?' Rodney began to ask Theodora guardedly, as they had all walked back.

'I can't *think* –' confessed Theodora naïvely. And indeed she had never hoped this, even of Laurel.

Hermione, swinging from Theodora's arm, put in eagerly: 'Uncle Edward looks as though he had had a fit, or come for a funeral. He didn't pay for the fly – shall we have to? I rushed out, of course, and said "Kiss me, Godfather!" and he said, "Not just now, Hermione" – he is always very polite – and sort of patted me, but I wasn't there. Mother came out and said, "My *dear* Edward!" That was when he didn't pay the fly. He said, "It's all right," and she said "Is Laurel ill?" and he said, "No, I've come for the children." I said, "They've gone – they're having their hair cut with Grandmother and Uncle Considine." He said, "What do you mean?" and I said he should just have seen them! – Shouldn't he just have seen them, Theodora? – Then Mother said to me not to get excited, so I went in and sat in the hall.'

'I offered him a drink,' said Theodora.

'Quite right.'

'But he wouldn't.'

'Oh?' said Rodney. And they had all felt, the two young women delightedly, as though they were hurrying in before a storm. But in this case the storm lay ahead.

'Poor Anna won't be here for the Nursing Fête. She had bagged the bran dip,' said Hermione.

'I daresay he'll change his mind,' said Rodney, but not quite confidently.

'I suppose *I'll* have to look after the bran dip now. But I shall be raffling the goat *and* selling buttonholes.'

'Don't chatter, Hermione.'

'But it will be awkward, won't it, Father; it will be awkward, won't it be? Unless I do the goat with the dip and give up the buttonholes. It's a milch one.'

'Yes, it will be awkward.'

'Has Anna been doing something perfectly awful? He *was* in a state.'

Edward's possible state in mind, Rodney had approached the library door with some apprehension. But no doubt it would be all right: one could rely on anyone, up to a point. Edward would be unlikely to refuse a drink for the second time. Or failing that, there would soon be tea. (Now what *had* fussed him? He had been sitting on all this for a week.) Janet with unfailing tact would have ordered tea early. And Rodney, having heartily shaken hands, should be able to say, 'Ah, tea! Good . . .'

Actually, on coming into the library he found Edward in what seemed his usual state of quite equable nervousness, failing to light a cigarette; Janet, ever so little preoccupied, one hand full of paper, was searching for the waste-paper basket on the wrong side of her table. 'To your left,' said Rodney, surprised. Then she shook in her handful of fine blue scraps, household notepaper. Rodney thought she and Edward must have been composing a difficult letter to someone together, then given up.

'And how is Laurel?' said Rodney.

'Oh, feeling the heat rather.'

'Pity she didn't come down with you.'

'Well, the fact is, Rodney, as I've been explaining to Janet, Laurel is anxious for various reasons to have the children back with us . . .'

'Taking them back?' said Rodney. 'That seems a pity . . .'

'Oh, it *is* a pity,' agreed Edward warmly. 'You've given them a marvellous time.'

Rodney's eyes sought Janet's, but she refused to confer. She went to the window. Directly Considine tried to come in she must send him out again with a message. Or would this have already occurred to Elfrida? At all events, one was alert for the car. Should she send Hermione out to intercept them? She stooped to the writing-table, hesitated, jotted a message, tore the sheet from her block. For a moment more Rodney's eyes implored her back; then, as though she had said 'Go away,' he returned his attention to Edward without resentment.

'Hermione'll be disappointed,' he said. 'They've got so many things on for next week – Look here, why not spare Laurel a few days to come and join them?'

'I'm afraid that's impossible,' said Edward regretfully.

Janet implied by the slightest possible movement: 'Don't make things difficult.'

'Just how you feel, of course,' said Rodney to Edward; and: 'Then what about tea, Janet?'

'I forgot,' said Janet surprisingly, and moved to the door. Rodney could not fail to detect, someone had been a victim. 'You look tired,' he said, forgetting Edward, following her a step or two.

'No – Then half-past six for the car, Edward?'

'She does look tired,' said Edward quickly. He sat down himself, when she left the room, overpowered by the very idea of her tiredness, and, as though he could at least do this for her, even relaxed a little. But he felt as though he had screamed and might scream again. To have screamed, in fact – he thought as he sat relaxed – would be a simplification. And better anything than to consider this new question of his and her relations; now printed out so neatly, confidently for his attention like a clause in an agenda. The question posed itself with an unbearable simplicity. At present, here they were; it was four o'clock and there seemed little to say to his brother-in-law. Here was Rodney indoors because of him at an extraordinary hour – this and Edward's dark suit projected a kind of Sabbath abnormality, a full stop grateful to neither. Naturally, nothing could be discussed. Rodney, re-crossing his legs, remained very solid and impermeable; passive, he put up a strong suggestion that nothing was sudden, nothing a pity, that it was unlikely anything had occurred. He grumbled gently to Edward about their visitors. It did not matter, but Lady Elfrida tore pieces out of *The Times* before it reached one – had Edward suffered? And Theodora played the piano at half-past one.

'At lunch?' said Edward stupidly.

'No, at night. I suppose it comes from living so much abroad. The piano's just under our room.'

'Can't you thump on the floor?'

'Yes, I do thump on the floor. But one can't help liking her.'

'I can,' said Edward.

'Of course, she has no sense of time – Look here, must you really go up by this train?'

'The seven-five? Yes – thanks very much, Rodney – we must, Laurel will be expecting us.'

It was clear, thought Edward, Janet thought Edward infantile; enemy to love because he had not loved herself. Conviction with or without resentment had been her note in their interview. Turning from this, he foresaw the hot return journey and, from this distance of a hundred or so miles, Laurel. They had seldom been, spatially, so divided. Proximity was their support; like walls after an earthquake they could fall no further for they had fallen against each other.

But apart from this necessity of never being divided, Laurel remained delicious. She made of every failure in peace, every break in their confidence a small burlesque. She despised balance, but her very wildness of thought, behind the propriety of her manner, seemed to insure them against catastrophe. There was nothing she could not bring to harmless light by exaggeration. When her accounts did not balance she said: 'You must marry Janet.' She reproached him for not going into business when he reproached her with wearing artificial pearls, wished that he had a mistress when love was not mutual, scrapped with Anna when she should have controlled her, exclaiming: 'I cannot think who can have had this impossible child!' She woke him at three in the morning to assure her her hair was not fading. Still, she would not condone his mother's infidelity to his childhood; they went to sleep hand-in-hand, she made up arrears of nonsense right back to his infancy and, though she frequently wept or was difficult, never turned an obdurate face away. If she was not serene she was gay and professed to find in Edward the spring of her comfort. Her solicitude reached him almost before he suffered, fostering sensibility. 'And life after all,' thought Edward, hearing tea approach, the gay dance of china on the silver tray, 'is an affair of charm, not an affair of passion.'

'Here they come!' said Rodney, relieved. They both heard the car turn with the drive and come up through the beeches. 'I expect they'll be glad . . .'

But Edward, who must be on wires, shot up and said he would go for a turn. Should Rodney have kept him? Edward was gone already, away down the drive. He must have gone to meet them. Rodney looked out at the dark-and-light damasky stripes of the lawn. Tomorrow they would be wanting one of his men for the motor lawn mower – the polite side of life was a constant tax. Rodney sighed: there went Edward again. One had done all one could.

But Lady Elfrida and the children, hopefully waving, saw Edward swerve off through the trees, like wild life away from the camera; one shadow more in the shadowy net.

'Dear me,' said Anna, 'he thinks we are callers.'

Lady Elfrida, as the car took the last turn of the drive, looked up anxiously at the house. Had it all been shocking? She braced herself to dash in and extricate Janet and Rodney from the wreckage

99

of habit. 'It's all right,' she told Considine; the untruth was mechanical. She brought out her powder-puff, turned her face this way and that in the small mirror's compass. 'Let the children get out,' she added, 'here comes Hermione.'

Considine's niece came rushing, the very spirit of an alarm. 'Mother says to take this to the village,' she shouted, mounting the running-board. And to Lady Elfrida: 'Please, Father says *come*: Mr Gibson is on the telephone!' Considine pulled up a moment to let them all out, then whirled round the sweep and was off again. The party dispersed all ways, to meet the emergency. In the dark hall, Lady Elfrida pulled off her gloves to telephone. But Theodora was there before her.

'But what do you *want*?' she kept saying.

'Oh, *you*, Theodora?' said Lewis, depressed.

'I'm afraid you can't speak to Janet.'

'But I hear Edward is with you; I wanted –'

'I can't tell you much,' went on Theodora, 'but you can ask questions; I'll say yes and no.'

'But look here, I really just wanted to speak to Edward.'

'– I don't think I should –'

'Look here, I've got a trunk call: I do wish you'd look for him.'

Theodora looked guardedly round the hall. 'You can imagine,' she said, 'how things are here . . .'

'But it struck me –'

'– It what? I'm afraid it's not much good your trying to speak to anyone, Lewis; your line's so bad. I can hardly hear you myself.'

'But I don't *want* –'

'Don't shout, Lewis; don't get so excited – I don't know what's the matter with Lewis,' she said to Lady Elfrida, who, in a state of unusual indecision, stood opposite herself in a dark looking-glass – Did a face launch ships?

'What *does* he want, Theodora?'

'He's quite unable to say.'

'How useless,' said Lady Elfrida, and took the receiver. Hearing Lewis continue from the inane, 'It struck me that just conceivably –' she cut in with 'My dear Lewis, you can't: it's useless; we none of us can,' and rang off. Through the house, up the stairs, the funny confined repetitions of crisis continued: she heard Anna quarrelling with Hermione. Then Janet called: 'Oh, be quiet, be *quiet!*' and came through the swing door with the Tilney children's overcoats on her arm. She was packing up.

'Has anyone seen Edward?' she said at once. 'Tea will be in in a moment.' Elfrida said she would find him, and went out.

'Darling . . . ?' said Theodora to Janet.

'Well?'

'You don't look very pleased.'

With unfriendly patience, Janet tried to get past Theodora to the stairs.

'*Janet*: look at me!'

'Please, Theodora . . . I'm packing up the children.'

'My God, why won't you look at me?'

'I see you so much,' said Janet wearily.

'I won't let you pass!' exclaimed Theodora helpfully, blocking the stairs. 'There must be some misunderstanding. Where can we talk?'

'Tea is just coming in.'

'Tea here is always just coming in. You make me perfectly wild —'

'Evidently,' said Janet. She turned back through the door and went up the back stairs. She longed for kindness — anyone's. Soundlessly weeping, she dropped a glove of Anna's and groped for it. Someone began to come out through a door saying: 'If you please —' She stumbled and went on up, quickly, brushing her shoulder against the lime-washed wall. 'I could have borne anything —' she thought, pushing open a door.

Meanwhile, 'Tea, Edward, tea!' called Lady Elfrida, crossing the lawn in his direction. Edward halted, stared, and came out into the glare to meet her. His dark moving figure against the trees was hardly clear to her, but his contracted smile seemed very high up: she never took his height into full account.

'Why did you run away?' she asked briskly.

'There were so many of you,' he said, at his most disarming.

'Well, as you know, a good many of us are staying here.' – She thought, 'And all wicked.' They met, smiled – for they seldom kissed – and turned together back to the house. The bold, hard façade stared them out – the house remained Considine's own. Edward perceived that his mother would not, after all, ask: 'What *is* the matter?' Something retarded her manner, though she was not subdued.

However, he took the defensive quickly, to crown the impossible afternoon. 'I can't really discuss –'

'How are you?' she asked, irrelevant.

'I don't want to make things difficult –'

'Then, my dear,' she exclaimed with one of her flashes, 'you do set the most curious way about it!'

'About what?'

'Don't let's argue – this is all too wretched!'

'Is it?' he asked. They halted.

'Naturally – *look* at all this!' But her quick gesture was for the present only. Confusion: she embraced the whole and seemed for the moment to suffer it, solitary. 'I must say,' she added, 'I think it's hard on the children.'

'They've got to come away sometime; they can't live here. What you mean really,' he said, 'is, it's hard on Janet.'

'Yes, you are at all times, Edward, miserably hard.'

'Do you think she thinks so?'

'How can I tell; why ask me? She may never think of it,' she exclaimed, impatient for herself and her sex. She implied: 'It's impossible to be anything but indifferent.' She put a hand through his arm, they moved on towards the house. She leaned on his arm, walking slowly and even dragging a little. As much as to say: 'One is always glad of this, all the same,' with a tenderness she could not express more happily. Or perhaps, in a little burlesque like Laurel's, trying on old age, parodying the future, hinting 'This is how I should like us to be,' rehearsing the impossible. The banks were steep: 'Pull me up, Edward.'

'Must we go in at once?'

'Oh, yes; tea's waiting.'

Rodney, watching the Tilneys come up the slope together, thought: 'It will be all right now, I expect.' But Lady Elfrida looked tired. For the first time, Rodney indicted Considine.

8

Considine had foretold a change of weather. By the time the empty car returned from the station, as they all sat down to dinner – diminished by quite a large number though Edward had not been thought of this time yesterday and the children were never with them at this hour – he was glad to be able to point out a film coming over the sky. The day would be shortened by quite an hour. Trees gave out a perceptible chill, the burnished landscape held an effect of after-glow from a week, a season, a finished eternity, more than a day. Rodney said one could do with some rain now, to which Lady Elfrida gave quite a meek assent.

The whole party was in disgrace with Theodora, who did not speak throughout dinner. Considine, with his annoying dry innocence, observed: surely this had been sudden? Surely a cloud of dust? Later, he and Theodora went off to play billiards. Janet had had the drawing-room fire lit, so Rodney who perfectly amiably did not wish for a fire sat in the library. The party had certainly broken up.

In the drawing-room, Elfrida drew up her gold shawl round her shoulders, gratefully approaching hands and person to the pink, delinquent summer firelight.

'Cold?' said Janet, with whom she was now alone.

'It will soon be very cold.'

'But you're shivering now.'

Mortality; a little autumn. 'Edward, you know,' said his mother, laconic.

Janet looked round the drawing-room; she could have wished they were not alone. She recalled that afternoon ten years ago when, in Trevor Square, Lady Elfrida had picked up in singular speculation the hand wearing Rodney's ring – which Janet still wore: an ageless diamond.

'They will soon be home now,' said Janet, looking up at the clock. 'That's the best train in the day.'

'He doesn't deserve it.'

In her deep chair, Janet sat upright, her hand spread out on the arm, as though expecting at any time to be called away. Though Elfrida looked at the fire Janet was aware of her close observation, a kind of violence. She said quickly, to interpose something: 'I hear Lewis rang up?'

'Oh yes, poor Lewis; no one would let him speak.'

'Perhaps he'll ring up again.'

'– My dear, you've let me make you a great deal of trouble.'

'It's not really so frightful.'

'Isn't it? *This* is a fiasco.'

Elfrida's 'this', though moulded by her long ring-laden fingers
into a very small kernel of, as it were, intensive action, or pain,
remained so comprehensive that Janet could not tell how far she
ought to look back. With impassive docility she lent herself to
the retrospect. She looked back to her very first sight of Edward,
to what had been a false dawn for her, then at his wedding half
in the rain. She looked beyond him steadily at the old branching
sin that like the fatal apple-tree in a stained-glass window had in
its shadow, at each side, the man and woman, Considine and
Elfrida, related only in balance for the design. And in her confused thought this one painted tree associated itself, changed to
another, the tree of Jesse; that springing – not, you would think,
without pain somewhere – from a human side, went on up flores-
cent with faces, perplexed similar faces, to some bright crest or
climax or final flowering to which they all looked up, which was
out of Janet's view. If you felled the tree, or made even a vital
incision, as Elfrida impatient of all this burden now seemed to
desire (for if her heart were the root, it had contracted, if hers were
the side, it ached), down they all came from the branches and
scattered, still green at the core like July apples, having no more
part in each other at all: strangers.

'I can't speak for you,' said Janet. 'I know it has been dreadful.
But none of us all can alter anything: this is how we have grown.'

Elfrida said hardily: 'Of course I am always ruined: one can't
be more. But look what I did to Edward, look how I scared him.
He's fit for no one but little Laurel –'

'You offend me rather,' said Janet abruptly.

'Nursery tea,' said Elfrida with, on Janet's behalf, her full
bitterness, an access of her most 'impossible' manner. But contemplating that miniature happiness in Royal Avenue she
softened, putting out in contrition a hand her Janet recognized
but could be relied upon not to take.

Janet, aware of the hand's intention, knew that if Elfrida had
not adored as a sort of sacred disqualification her Janet's stupidity,
she must have despised Janet. As it was, Elfrida was irritated
enough. For she had gone too far, she had relied on today's
explicit awkwardness to precipitate something; perhaps expecting
even to find Janet in Edward's arms – nature as well as circumstance having made her conceive of love as a very high kind of
overruling disorder, she hoped much of any break with the

amenities. As for Rodney, Laurel, the children begotten in error, finance, position, the two establishments, these did not, clearly, present themselves to Elfrida. For her own part, such attachments had withered too long ago, leaving so many scars along the stem. She had brought up, perhaps, to meet today's crisis, some nebulous if profound idea of herself as ministering everywhere, consoling, adopting, shedding her own impatient clarity on any possible stupefaction or loss. She was opposed, however, to explanation in any form: this love of Janet's became an affair of her own passionate continuity. 'The trouble is,' thought Janet, 'that I cannot think and Elfrida won't.'

'You did talk, Janet? Theodora said you and Edward had a long talk in the library.'

'I said he was so foolish about the children.'

'The children? – Nonsense, Janet, of course he loves you.'

Janet, after a pause, said: '*You* were the reason I married Rodney.'

Lady Elfrida received this blankly. She made an extravagant gesture of astonishment, which was not enough. Putting her hands up to screen herself from the fire she leaned back and looked round the room behind her, at the cabinets and curtains, for many witnesses. Then returning, speechless, to Janet, she implied a whole range of new curiosity. Her look burnt itself out on those downcast eyelids.

'Oh, so you had known all the time, from the first, about Considine?'

'Oh yes, I'd heard once; why should I forget? When I went to stay with Margaret, I thought, "This is near where *he* lives." His name was the name of the county to me – written large like that – of course I wanted to come here. It seemed extraordinary Mother and Father should not remember: of course, we had never discussed you.'

'– I must have been the only possible pity about Edward –'

'No, Mother and Father don't talk when they're comfortable. Why should they ask? They knew nothing was Edward's fault. But I thought to myself, "How can they not remember *his* name?" And Batts – it seemed a whole part of England. But they liked me to go to Margaret's; it was a change, you see.'

'Yes, it was nice for you.'

'When we came to Batts to tennis that afternoon I could hardly speak. But it rained, you know. Margaret thought me so stupid, I suppose I was rather. Considine seemed a rather bad host that afternoon; we were not his sort, of course.'

'What did you think . . . ?'

'I – he was smaller than I expected.'

'Yes, he's smaller than I remember.'

'He seemed a little . . . indistinct. Rodney was really more like what –'

'So you've married them both.'

'It seemed *something* for me – I wanted to be related. I suppose that seems odd to you – I can see now it was odd,' said Janet, with her calm precision.

'So you took Rodney –' Her friend re-examined the situation from this angle. 'Of course,' she added, 'it is extraordinary to me that a woman as little cold as you are should keep so quiet.'

'It was a question of what I wanted – couldn't you have kept quiet once?'

'We're not speaking of passion,' returned Elfrida impatiently. '*This* was – determination. Perhaps that's the only passion you have – Are you guileful, Janet?'

'I don't know. Am I?'

'Had you really forgotten Edward's –? Didn't you realize . . .?'

'I meant him to notice me.'

'Did you? I suppose one does – I'd forgotten.'

'I suppose – if I thought – I knew I should make him angry. I thought we might all feel better afterwards; I didn't know it would last. You see, I had no experience, nothing outside myself.'

'They all thought – poor bewildered dears – you were simply perverse.'

'I know. But all I thought (then at first) was, "Here is a place for me." You see, what had gone wrong with me about Edward was so difficult to – so unreasonable; it was impossible to understand. I felt at a loss; it was like being idle with a wrist broken or something when I had always been able to use my hands and be so busy. It felt awkward, like not knowing what to do on the stage; like when I was once given a small part in some acting because it was so very small, they thought too small even for me to spoil. No one explained the part to me, so I stood there with no words to say and nothing to do with my hands. Do you see what I mean, Elfrida? It was like that – I don't suppose that has ever happened to you – so when Rodney came it was like being given directions. And he was so kind. I felt sure I was right – didn't you, one time?'

'– No, *I* felt sure I was happy. That can never be contradicted, even afterwards.'

'I thought I could do what was natural. I never thought, you know, of being *opposed* to Edward. I knew we must all be young, though I didn't feel like that, and that we were bound to grow, and I thought there must be some kind of strength in growing, like a plant has, that pushes things, even paving-stones, out of the way and grows past them. I thought being afraid or angry were like stones; I didn't see they had a life of their own and made growth too, and could be so strangling –'

'And I thought you never thought!'

'This is how I see it now; at the time I did what I had to do; there must have been some reason. When you're in despair, Elfrida –'

'By now, how wrong do you think you were?'

'You see, I haven't often looked back.'

'I suppose you're not good exactly. But you're certainly at some disadvantage.'

'I've always felt so,' said Janet.

Elfrida gathered the bright, metallic folds of her shawl in a quick movement. She reconsidered this strange desire of Janet's to be related. 'She is – she's frightening,' she thought. 'I see what Edward –'. Herself, loved as she loved: to extinction, she had never exercised this dark power.

'You see what it is,' she said. 'Edward started ahead of us all – from when he was five, from when I – Something was always owed him; no one could ever slap him. For my part, of course, I could not slap anybody; from that point, I lost my hold; I couldn't even dismiss a servant. Never to be in the right – it's the only possible ruin, I daresay, if one's nothing besides a woman. You can have no idea of it, Janet. For instance, when I was first in Paris my money – credit stopped, for a few days: there'd been some mistake. I couldn't order things at a shop – you have no idea. I used to sit down to meals thinking "I ought not to." It really was destitution;. I'd never been without some kind of a moral privilege. And for some time after I'd been – put away – I hated signing my name on a cheque. You see I wasn't really a

Tilney. I kept out of debt for more than a year, answered letters, felt wretchedly friendly to everyone; I met my cook in one of my own dresses and never said anything. I was grateful when anyone trod on my toe and apologized. Being shady, Janet – of course in those days I was full of vanity – it was like losing one's looks.'

Janet thought: 'I wish she wouldn't –' She exclaimed: 'How dark it is!'

'I suppose it's midnight – No, look, a quarter to ten. Do you think they're still in the billiard-room? He really must beat Theodora.'

'Who must?' Janet said vaguely.

'Considine, naturally,' Elfrida said in the dark, sharply. 'Oh, is it true she wrote such a nasty letter?'

'Who said –?'

'She did; she said to me she supposed that must be the matter. How odd she is, poor thing; quite a dark horse. Well, not so dark really, blotchy. But you know Considine's no good at any game, he doesn't care enough; bored. I could beat him at billiards, always. He keeps humming and chalking his cue. Those days – at one time – I used to wake up at three o'clock; it was a sort of rendezvous, when the clock struck; I'd rather have been asleep, but anyway, there I always was – to watch him do little silly things over and over again in my head, in the dark. In one's head, I suppose, or else they had never stopped, somewhere; been going on all the time: something to do with one's eyes. Fumbly little things, never very well done; a cue being chalked, a cigarette being rolled; "God Save the King" being played with his left hand on the back of his right. Or a hansom being stared at until it stopped; then he'd give the man half a crown and say "No, let's walk." Tricks, ways of doing things you know, they madden one at the beginning. They pull something right out taut; one thinks "Perfection". They're the most precious exasperations, until exasperation itself sets in. One thinks of them to smile, one can safely smile in the dark; they're all one has left of oneself, the pleasure one won't share. Then suddenly – every night – something goes, all the pleasure. "I never saw you: I'll never see you again!" To get back, you have to remember everything through again, like a lesson. Or like something you've once been told – Well, the darkness is changed every night, nothing stays on it. What a mercy, Janet!'

'I've never smiled like that – I never could.'

'No? Then last thing you turn over, hear your eyelashes on the pillow and something hammering inside the pillow, think, "Here *I* still am." Then when you wake next morning the tide's right out, you could weep. Then there's a letter – How much too much I do talk, Janet!'

'Perhaps I don't understand – Oh, what's that?'

'Where?' cried Elfrida, startled.

'Listen!'

'Hermione...'

The call, any call, for which Janet had been alert. She made for the door quickly, drawing shadow after her black dress. Elfrida sighed. Janet's distance even from love made her enigmatic when indeed she was not enigmatic at all but a plain woman. You pulled her guard away, she appeared to offer herself frankly but was immediately disembodied. Now she was off to comfort a little girl's night fears. Lady Elfrida had no nervous life, her nerve was the heart; she turned all the lights on in angry solitude. 'I'm old,' she thought. 'I'm beginning to raven; I can't bear people to go away.' She sought her own face for reassurance, repaired it, ran a finger-tip over the eyebrows and crossed the hall to seek company. They were coming out of the billiard-room. She met Considine, smaller than she remembered.

Janet found Hermione shivering at a turn of the stairs. 'I had a frightful dream; I dreamed I was nowhere.'

Janet, kneeling, chafed the cold arms that were round her neck. 'You know you mustn't.'

'The house feels funny. Can't I stay down here with you?'

'That would never do.'

'I'm all inside my head. Can I have Gladys up to sing "Abide with me"? – Oh, then *you* abide with me, Mother; I'd much rather.' They returned to Hermione's room. 'My bed looks nice,' said Hermione, 'it's a wonder I don't enjoy it more. Doesn't Anna's bed look empty!'

'Curl up tight and think about your dormouse. Think of poor people in trains with nothing to lean on – there's a train now.'

'It's frightfully far away. Do you think it really *is* a train? Will Anna be home now?'

'I expect so, and sound asleep.'

'Oh, go on holding me tight, don't go; I wish we were the same person!'

'Let's tell each other about Friday week, about the Nursing Fête.'

'You talk, Mother; you tell me.'

Janet, her arms across the pillow, said: 'Well, there'll be the band. And you know, they'll be running those blue motor-buses from Market Keaton. There will be hundreds of people there, Hermione. Did I tell you Cousin Dolores was lending her decorations? There will be flags enough to go twice round the tea tent. You must be sure to go down with flowers that morning and help Mrs Robertson arrange the vases for the tea-tables.'

'Secretly, the cakes we send are always the nicest, aren't they? Mrs Robertson tells me so every year, but I say, "Oh no." You'll wear your dark red, won't you, Mother? How fine do *you* expect it will be?'

'I expect, very fine indeed.'

'And I expect, *frightfully* fine. But I hope there'll be wind enough for the flags. I hope there'll be Japanese flags with heaps of suns, and American flags too. I do think the Union Jack is boring, don't you, Mother. – Oh, and my goat! – Oh, I wish I could sleep till Friday week!'

'It'll soon be Friday.'

Janet turned the pillow; Hermione, her cheek to the cool new pillow, was practically asleep. Her arms loosened. Her face was close to a shining, slippery stream; she, stirring like that alive thing down in the leaves that she never discovered, shook the flat bright leaves above her to someone else's astonishment. She was hidden like a corncrake, distant like a cuckoo, close like a nesting swallow under the roof. She came up once through the hollow strong stems, knocking light from the leaves to murmur: 'It's almost next day.'

Presently Janet could creep away.

Part III
Wednesday

I

Mrs Thirdman was in town for the day, for the sales. She arrived a little before Laurel at Laurel's club, which was remarkably central. The portico was imposing; Willa slipped past the alert maroon pages and chaste bronze grill with a distinct sense of privilege. The house had a past and a name: on the white stone, high-windowed staircase the shadow of a branch raised ducal ghosts for her. Arch after arch, the reception-rooms were extensive, impassive; here a great flood of furniture was arrested. To place oneself was distracting; to be claimed by Laurel one must be well in evidence. Willa side-glanced this way and that at members sitting rather gloomily in abeyance. She slipped off a glove, then slipped it on again.

Now Alex had for years been urging Willa to join one of these ladies' clubs. He feared that she might be missing something. She thought, perhaps one *was* missing something. For here, besides giving lunch and even dinner to friends – and the waiters would be accustomed to taking orders from ladies, would make allowance, no doubt, for some slight hesitation, and there would be gentle curries and nice little egg dishes – she could rest, wash her hands, see the weekly papers and have her parcels delivered. And: 'Meet me at my club,' she would be able to say. At some clubs, she had heard, one could exhibit one's water-colours, there was a strong cultural element, they had debates on subjects and interesting people spoke . . . This might even attract Theodora.

Willa got so far as projecting a little lunch party: Mr Gibson, Alex, herself and the interesting chaplain from Vevey's kind wife. But she had arrived today a little dishevelled and sticky from pulling dresses on and off over her head at Peter Robinson's. She knew Laurel would turn up looking like a tea-rose. So directed by a page she went down to wash, among glass and marble. She felt some apprehension, uncertain that the accommodation provided might not be for members alone – this brilliant white marble vault, the hinged mirrors reflecting a thousand profiles, the cut-glass bowls of salmon-pink powder, the cut-glass trays of cotton-wool tufts to puff powder on with, the pins, the brushes. So she turned off the hot tap almost at once, just ran the cold tap over her wrists, and made use of a towel left by a clean-looking lady rather than take a fresh one. Meanwhile, two members swung up their feet on to two *chaises-longues* and, beginning to buff their nails, exchanged medical confidences. Treatment ... there seemed to be nothing nowadays you could not get done. Of course they could not know Willa was not a member. But did they even know she was a married woman? One blush, brilliant under the artificial daylight, and Willa fled, with hat, scarf and handbag. Then she had to come creeping back again for her gloves.

Upstairs again Willa, fresh but chastened, sat down in an arm-chair broad as an elephant's back that stared all over with bougainvillea and jade-green jays – one of fifty chairs all so attired. She supposed this would be a modern cretonne, not suitable for a cottage room? It would not have been suitable in Switzerland either, but might have looked well in the South of France. It might look well at Batts, perhaps, but Rodney was said to be so conservative, and Theodora complained that Janet would not oppose him. The jays would not have done, of course, in any room with a parrot. But she could not imagine wanting to keep a parrot. Among the armchairs there were a great many glass-topped tables. Till just now, the *Tatler* and the *Sketch* had been spread about on them with a great air of munificence, but a member had come with a fierce look, swept these all up and carried them off with her to a corner divan. There, though she could not look at more than two at a time, she hid the others behind the cushions ... This left only the ashtrays: Willa did not smoke.

'*Oh*,' cried Laurel, 'it's shocking I'm so late! I've no idea what becomes of me!' She slid through the chairs in a cool smiling rush and sat down to proclaim her despair. Had poor dear Willa arrived without difficulty? Had she had a frightful morning too?

'Your club is so central,' said Willa gratefully.

'But not for anywhere that I ever am – Have you been shopping? How terrible for you. How nice this is! It's ages – One thing, – Mother's later than I am: she loses her head, you know. And Mrs

Bowles? – Oh, Willa, it is so dreadful about Mrs Bowles; I hope you will understand,' said Laurel earnestly. 'But if you'd been Elfrida herself I still couldn't have avoided her. You see, we use Mrs Bowles as a kind of annex when Mother and Father are up, because you see we have no spare room, with all our children and things. And that does have to mean a good deal of pleasantness and at least one lunch. I can't have her to dinner because of Edward. And yet somehow when Elfrida has Janet with her it's the other way round, Elfrida feels she ought to be pleasant to *me* and ask *me* to lunch and everything and it's so unnatural. Life is difficult, isn't it?'

'Mrs Bowles?' said Willa.

'You see, I'm afraid she's coming to lunch with us.'

Laurel paused, waved to a page and offered Willa a bronx. 'Though they're horrid here,' she said, 'warm.' Willa, impressed, said she did not think she should care for a bronx, even a warm one. Laurel did not feel that, under the circumstances, she need ask after Theodora. It was really a wonder, the other day, that Edward had not died. With an ever-recurrent amazement, she eyed dear sensitive Willa. How *could* she and Alex ...? It must have been something pre-natal. Perhaps Willa had been to an unpleasant play. Laurel herself had been most careful, before Anna and Simon were born; she took no chances. She did hope, now, she had been successful with Willa and seemed to establish a kind of a league of youth. She would have hated Willa to think Laurel thought her a 'Mrs Bowles person'. Laurel could not help knowing that had any combination of, say, Elfrida and Mrs Bowles been really in question, she would have had herself wired for to the country or gone to bed for the day.

Mrs Studdart appeared, with Mrs Bowles who seemed pleased to be with them. Mrs Studdart expressed surprise at Laurel's punctuality. 'I do wish,' she said affectionately to Willa, 'that Sussex were not so far from Cheltenham.' They moved into the dining-room. 'Lunch will be beastly,' said Laurel, fanning herself with the menu. 'I don't think there's anything I can recommend. Shall we all have melon?'

Sunblinds were dark against the glare of the street and electric punkahs in motion, but it was certainly hot.

'I always admire your frescoes,' said Mrs Bowles, looking up at the ceiling wreathed with goddesses.

'Surely,' said Mrs Studdart, 'frescoes are only frescoes if they are on a wall?'

'How is Edward?' said Willa to Laurel, with gentle eagerness.

'Oh, feeling the heat rather. How is Alex?'

'Gardening; it is so good for him.'

'I wish Edward gardened.'

Mrs Studdart asked: 'How is Theodora?'

'Oh, so well, after her lovely week at Batts! They are all so good,' said Willa expansively.

'Still studying music?' said Mrs Studdart vaguely. She had no idea what Theodora did, and as a rule thought it better not to inquire.

'She hasn't much time,' said Willa proudly.

'She's such an interesting girl,' interposed Mrs Bowles. 'She always seems to me so unusual.'

'Poor Willa's been shopping.'

'Of course, I never shop in the sales,' said Mrs Studdart. 'You can never be sure. I have just come up to go to some theatres. But it's a curious thing, it's always the plays I have seen that come to Cheltenham.'

'I always think this is such a magnificent dining-room,' said Mrs Bowles, while Laurel waved away the waiter who was trying to bring them soup. 'We don't want soup,' she said. 'Do we? How fearful food is: I'm so glad I'll soon be in Brittany.'

'Brittany?' exclaimed Willa.

'I mean, I'm sick of this club.'

'But we heard you would all be going to Batts,' said Willa.

'Oh, hadn't you heard? We thought after all we would take the children somewhere to play on the rocks. Edward hears now Brittany's too picturesque, but we'd taken our rooms and everything.'

'Oh, I *quite* understood you were going to Batts,' said Willa, distressed. 'I heard they were all expecting you.'

'Well, they aren't expecting us now,' said Laurel cheerfully. 'Janet quite understands. We offered to take Hermione, but they thought better not. As it is, we hope Anna and Simon may play with French children.'

'French has certainly been an advantage to Theodora,' said Mrs Bowles faithfully. Laurel's bright quick look went round the table and hung in space a moment with a pensive tilt of the eyelids.

114

Her thoughts fled by like water, as elusive, spinning their own shadow. With a composed movement, a ghost of Janet's, she once more took up the menu. 'Sole, I think?' she said.

But Mrs Studdart looked at her sharply. As on that wedding morning when rain tapped and trickled, the ices were uncertain, the lilies had not been delivered, she attributed much to Edward. It had never before rained for one of Laurel's parties. Mrs Studdart tried hard to recall some shafts of bitterness, now in full flight. But Laurel's brilliance worried her, like electric light burnt too extravagantly. She thought happy women dulled a little, something crept over them . . . Now surely it was reckless of them to be going to Brittany? Batts would have been more human, more economical. 'You will have to be careful about the milk,' she said, with the air of reserving much. It became plain to Mrs Thirdman and Mrs Bowles, something must have occurred and be still occurring. Estrangement, friction? Was it Rodney, was it Edward? Marriage was always difficult.

'I hear Batts is delightful,' said Mrs Bowles.

'I expect you can swim, Laurel?' asked Willa.

'You must not miss Mont St Michel,' said Mrs Bowles.

So far, Laurel considered, it had not been a bad day with Mrs Bowles, but at this point her mother's friend refilled her water glass, broke up another roll and leaned forward to tell them about her expedition to Mont St Michel. Laurel's manner went quite to pieces; she absented herself like a child that has asked, 'May I get down?' her chin drooped, her eye wandered, once or twice she looked up at the brim of her hat. Yet as Mrs Bowles' story continued, gathering years of such talk on its vigorous dullness as on a running-thread, Laurel's nostalgia for girlhood became acute. Her 'teens – their exposure to stingless boredom, their extravagant reverie; a home that gave her life colour, taking none of her life's; the cool ball-dress slipping over her arms; her impatient stitching of summer dresses, their lyric wearing. Janet and Mother tacking roses on to her bodice (it would be a wonder if someone did not propose tonight), Mrs Bowles' voice ran on. So the trees drowsed (a dull London sycamore crossed the window now) while Mrs Bowles talked and Laurel's reel of pink cotton rolled away underneath the piano; Laurel had to go flat on her stomach: Mr Bowles, on a visit, talked on: Laurel getting up bumped her head on the underneath of the keyboard and thought suddenly of Edward:

Mrs Bowles' words like rather old dulled fish gently tipped from a barrow went on slipping and slipping. She loved Edward; delicious uncertainty perished that moment before this voice. She recalled her father's affection, how he never listened to what she said, how at home, with mounting voices, they all talked for hours at cross purposes; with what ease one burst into angry tears. Quiet plumes of lilac, the band heard far down the Promenade; she relived the perpetual Cheltenham afternoon. At corners of white-walled residential roads, under lamps slung over the avenues, an immoderate pleasure had surprised her. To her share in all this she would, from her too pointed, too explicit relation with Edward, willingly have returned. Sheltering here and there in memories, as in doorways, from the storm of her present anguish – these weeks since Edward's return from Batts had been unadmittedly frightful – she saw the land behind her shadowless in the unreal light of regret. She was racked, she was extravagant in her sense of loss. A break with her now so ghostly present she did not contemplate. It was a maiden rather than widowed daughter who, in Corunna Lodge, looked out of the staircase window, with only the vaguest sense of having been absent, at the ever-cheerful poplars. All the same – she knew while Mrs Bowles still talked on – one could never bear it.

' – So the girls agreed we had better not,' Mrs Bowles was concluding. 'Naturally it was impossible to replace the thermos, but we had a little spirit lamp. A so-called "Tommy's cooker"; they are so practical; I have often made tea on one inside an attaché case on my knees in the train coming back from Italy. However, Angela quite blamed herself and insisted on going back to leave a message. She went back with Mrs Hamilton; they both went back to explain. You must remember, Laurel, they all speak *patois* in Brittany; it is not like French at all. Meanwhile Mildred and I were quite anxious; we thought of leaving a message with the stationmaster, but there was no stationmaster. However, just as the train came round the bend, Angela and Mrs Hamilton came driving up in a *fiacre*, waving triumphantly. Mrs Hamilton had taken the *fiacre*. Even so, they had to run down the platform; poor Mrs Hamilton quite breathless. I can assure you we were quite a sensation, and there was a good deal of perfectly good-natured fun. The train was packed; Mrs Hamilton so kindly insisted on paying supplement for herself and me: "old bones",

she said, so we travelled first. The girls love types, they preferred
to stand in the corridor. The hotel 'bus met us as we had arranged,
so altogether the day went off splendidly. We hope to see more
of Mrs Hamilton; she knows there is always our little prophet's
chamber. Laurel, you and Edward must certainly come to tea
before you go to Brittany; we could show you photographs, and
Angela could put Edward up to some little dodges about the
hotels. She is always the man of our party.'

'It all takes me back to Lausanne,' said Willa, sighing. Expedi-
tions were over, Alex's rucksack was put away; though they *went*
out they would not 'set out' any more. 'All the same,' she
thought, 'if I were Gertrude Studdart in London I'd stay at one of
those little hotels in the Cromwell Road. They are not expensive.'

'Mrs Bowles, it is dreadful for Edward, he can never go out to
tea –'

But a page came between the tables. All four felt some apprehension; Mrs Bowles, as though dug up from Pompeii, was
petrified in the act of wiping her mouth. Laurel pulled a sweet-
pea from a vase and sat twirling the gay winged flower. The
messenger, like death, approached. A call to the telephone? The
dark-gold, Olympic ceiling shut like a trap on some mild large
sky, a personal spaciousness into which, under the influence of
Mrs Bowles, they had all ascended, or all been dissolved; they
heard the loud hum of the club dining-room. 'For you, Laurel, I
daresay,' said Mrs Studdart, who hoped, feared, expected and
hardly liked to suppose ... Or was it that Edward habitually
telephoned at lunchtime?

'Mrs Meggatt is on the telephone.'

'*Janet?*'

'She's not in London?'

'She may be speaking from Batts.'

'That's not like Janet – how can she know where you are?'

Was this? ... Or was this? The three ladies looked away from
each other. They looked at Laurel's empty place with the chair
awry, the poor sweet-pea lying across her plate.

'I had no idea Janet was in town,' said Mrs Studdart. Less
communicative than ever, her dark daughter.

117

2

'Janet?'

'Laurel? I'm just up.'

'Oh, lovely – Where are you?' cried Laurel with an unaccountable quaver, shut in with her sister's voice in the strait little telephone box like a coffin upright.

'I'm having lunch with Edward, at the Ionides.'

'*Oh,* how nice!'

'I rang up your house and they didn't know where you were, so I rang up Edward and he said you were giving lunch to Mother and Willa at the club, so we thought he and I'd better lunch.'

'And Mrs Bowles is here, too.'

They laughed even more than this merited and arranged a meeting. Janet went back to Edward, from whom, as she crossed the Ionides under the fans, it was plain that she had already been absent too long.

The coffee had come; it was cooling. What could she have to say? Why speak *now*, at all, to Laurel? From now, he and she would not feel alone any more. His mind was no more than a clock where each minute struck like a little hour, with such a reverberation among his senses that the hum of the restaurant was retarded, the indoor light paled or darkened, damask coarsened to canvas as though some magnifying quality were in his touch. This clang of over-charged minutes pointed the irony of those years . . . Seeing her come, Edward poured out his coffee.

Janet, sitting down again, smiled across at Edward. She pulled a rose further into her buttonhole, shook her head at a cigarette, poured out her coffee. She appeared for the first time lovely, and infinitely disingenuous. He recalled the occasion – which with a silent naturalness, like a child's, had already taken its place in their common memory – when she had shown she loved him. He had to find her trustworthy.

'Was she there? You've been a long time.'

'They looked all over the club: I believe they're stupid.'

'Was she surprised?'

'She knew I wanted to see her before France.'

'Did she –?'

'There was no time. We are to meet in an hour, in Royal Avenue.'

'So after this I shan't see you.'

Janet said, with the little derisive smile of someone too idle to think, picking up a refrain: 'You should be coming to Batts. You know you will have to come some day.'

Edward said nothing. They exchanged a glance of extra-ordinary intimacy which was at the same time, on his part, feverish and unhappy. The naturalness of· their interview – throughout lunch, from the moment of meeting till now they had been easily brother and sister – in itself created a sense of emer-gency, of having been dwarfed into this very naturalness by some large event or presence, like birth or death. There had, it is true, been one or two vital interpolations, she had asked: 'But why were you afraid of me?' He had said, later: 'But look here; look, Janet, a mistake grows right into one's life, one can't attack it.' He more or less plainly confessed to a dread of love in the more searching of its implications, to a more than moral distaste for the cruel inconvenience, the inconvenient cruelty of passion. And meanwhile she looked at him with a terribly mild and profound, a penetrating non-comprehension that was the enemy of his spirit.

Now she was back he took up one of her gloves, turned it over, attempted something again. 'Yes?' she said, and sat with her hands crossed, reflective, sombre but with an air of being en-tranced. 'You were too . . . good,' he had to say finally.

'Better than you deserved, or than you wanted?'

'Than I wanted,' he said, with an agonized deliberation.

'You let me feel that; it was insulting.'

'But now that has gone,' he thought – seeing, as she sat there unconscious and immobile, her hands and the poise of her head – 'now what are we to live on?' For, never in oversight or con-fusion but with entire deliberation, what he had not loved had been her integrity. And if that virtue of wholeness had been simply a quality in her behaviour, if her present noble innocence in affection denied her nobility, light went out of the scene instantly; it became indifferent to him, in his groping, where he rested or if this hand he touched in the dark were indeed her own. Her very innocence, her unguardedness, the approach there was to ex-travagance in her slow, dark looking, the directness she brought

119

from her practical life to express passion, seemed in their present triumphant misuse to shadow decay, so that the whole bitterness of an unfruitful autumn was present in this belated flowering.

'I have never felt good,' she added.

To her sister, Janet had spoken the truth. Her lunching here with Edward today was an accident, and was without precedent. Duty, affection brought her to town, convention prompted his invitation: having parted, out on the steps at Batts, distracted relations, they met as lovers. For three weeks, since his return from Batts with the indignant children, Edward, hard-worked, *distrait*, prey to his own and Laurel's confusion, had thought very little and not been aware in himself of the operation of memory. A sort of emotional famine had set in in Royal Avenue. That glaringly bright afternoon at Batts, like some experiment with colour dabbed on the edge of a palette, was wiped out again. The day remained, with its date, the briefest diary jotting: exasperated by gossip he had hurried to Batts, had an interview with his sister-in-law marked by resentment on her part and some hysteria on his own, been quizzed by his mother and hurried away his children. A sheer expense of time he could ill afford.

There had been nothing to say, meanwhile: Edward and Janet had not communicated. For her part, Janet sent back, with some smocks of Anna's and shirts of Simon's home late from the wash, a glove of Edward's he had dropped in the hall. Anna wrote thanks to Rodney, Simon to Janet, and Laurel requested, in an inclusive letter of thanks, that if Edward had seemed not himself in any way they would remember he had been overworked for a year. Edward joined, she wrote, in her appreciation of their goodness. They had been angels – Did Janet know Considine gave children so many ices? Would that be likely to agree with Hermione? – And was Theodora still with them at Batts? She supposed, hardly.

'I'm afraid Laurel's worrying,' Janet had commented, passing across the letter.

Rodney loved Laurel, he hated to think this possible. 'Surely she needn't think we'd mind Edward if she doesn't. Tell her of course it's all right.'

'I think that might embarrass them.'

'Perhaps you're right. Well, they'll feel better when they're both here in July. Do you think Edward would like to help make the golf-course? Or, Hermione's very anxious to dredge the lake.'

'But, Rodney, Edward will be exhausted; he wants to rest.'

'I thought he might feel worse with nothing to do.'

Lady Elfrida said there had been enough Tilneys at Batts and had soon afterwards left them for Ireland. Theodora exclaimed to Janet: 'I can't stand this, you are an icicle!' and confounded by Rodney's politeness, Janet's lassitude and the approach of the Nursing Fête, went away impressively to re-open the flat. Here she commanded a visit from Lewis, mixed some powerful drinks and told him Edward had finally ruined himself with Janet. Lewis reported to Lady Elfrida in Ireland that Edward went about looking wretched over this Batts affair and Lady Elfrida wrote crossly of Edward to Janet that he was giving himself a nervous breakdown. Rodney advised Janet to discount almost all of this. Considine went abroad.

The Nursing Fête over, there had been an anticlimax; at Batts they began to look forward to the arrival of the Tilneys. Hermione, forgetting how little she liked Anna, crossed off the days on her calendar; her father promised that they should motor twice a week to the sea and bathe. So that news of a drastic change in the Tilneys' holiday plans was received with consternation.

'I don't think they'll like France *at all*. Do you, Mother? Do you think they'll like it?'

'You never know.'

'Oh, I'd hate it, I know. Old France!'

Janet wrote back at once to agree with Laurel that the Continent taken in this agreeable form should be at once stimulating to the children and soothing to Edward. Edward and Laurel had been right, *of course*, not to feel themselves bound. There was no question of anything more than a disappointment. Rodney and Janet perfectly understood; Rodney and Janet envied them. Those hot sands . . . And at Batts already the borders were going off; the delphiniums had been cut down to flower again in September. She wished all good progress to Anna and Simon's French, and had it half in her mind to send Laurel a cheque to buy cotton dresses. She would love, Janet knew, to look pretty, crisp, jaunty, un-English in Brittany; the deep-enough droop to the wide-enough hat, though on the sands beside her weary Edward might lie with his eyes closed. 'I only hope they can afford it,' Mrs Studdart had written.

Addressing this letter, Janet had thought: 'It is certainly for the best.' But when finding no stamps in her box, none in Rodney's, she had to send to the village, her spirit faltered. 'I am not, of course, to see Edward. But someday – surely we stay related? As I said once, there will be Christmas and everything . . . I'd like to have asked Elfrida.'

So that today, ten days later, she followed her letter to town. It had been her intention only to see Laurel. Rodney was sympathetic. Something had gone so wrong, or been so falsely seen, she and Laurel could hardly write to each other nowadays. Their letters read oddly: 'composed'. Here was pain, far-reaching, awkward, a distortion. When Laurel and she were together, unconsciously smiling, with everything, nothing to say, they so easily spoke it was hardly to speak at all. They must meet. For here, unthinkably, was suspicion.

These weeks, a grotesque, not quite impossible figure, had come to interpose between herself and Laurel. A woman, an unborn shameful sister, travestying their two natures, enemy to them both. Against her Laurel's derision, Janet's pride was powerless. She resembled each for the other, and pressing in between them since they had permitted themselves to part a little interposed a preposterous profile that to each, at the very edge of her vision, was somehow darkly familiar. 'Surely Laurel could not take her for me, or I for her Laurel?' Where had the three met, how did the two, innocent, recognize the third? We know *of* her, we do not know her. Never overt, less than a sinner, worlds apart from Elfrida, she was the prey of all speculation, the unpitiable quarry of talk. Laurel once said: 'Do you notice, it's always the same woman whose letters are read in court?' This ever-presence in profile had, for each of the sisters, the Egyptian effective defect: from Janet's side or from Laurel's – could either have seen her, she was so close, or, faced her, she was so dreadful – two eyes were visible, focused elsewhere with an undeviating intentness. The look directed upon Edward its whole darkness.

For Janet, used to a small range of thought and great clarity, this horrible illusory figure had materialized on the upward train journey. The porter shutting the door shut Janet in with it; while the train ran down through a cutting they shared darkness; while the carriage crossing the downs became a running box of light the figure, feeding on day itself, enlarged, took Janet within its outlines, occupied finally her own corner place. So much Janet that it drew on her every instinct for its defence; so much Laurel that she could not attack it.

Janet's dismay was formless. 'Surely,' she thought, looking out at herself – for the train running under a bank, the window became a mirror – 'there is nothing with me but what I am?'

'Today' – for the fields swam up again into broad morning – 'when Laurel and I are lunching together, this will be gone? Won't this be blown away? Where shall we lunch – I think we'll lunch out, somewhere cheerful: Laurel would like that. I shall be angry with her; really this idea of Brittany is absurd; it will be no kind of holiday with these wretched children. Really Laurel lives by exaggeration; she cannot bear to be calm. I shall say ... I shall make her see ... She began falling in love simply for fun, when she was fourteen. Those absurd photographs. There has never been anything Laurel couldn't say. Or perhaps there was never anything she *had* to say? No, I'm wrong; she was afraid before Anna was born and she never told me. So today, when we're lunching together ... Now, soon, in two hours, at lunch ...' A cold thought: 'Shall I find her? Ought I to have telephoned?'

It was inconceivable, later, that she should find Laurel missing from Royal Avenue, not to be traced. Janet was more than at a loss, she was shocked; she did not know what to do. She thought: 'Has she run away from me?' Then in her anger, a rare mood accustomed to govern and contravene any mood of Laurel's, she rang up her brother-in-law. With a shock, repeated, doubled in this new duality of her nature's, she heard Edward's voice. For him she had only one answer: she had come to London to see him.

So, meeting and smiling in the Ionides' door, they had mutely exchanged some countersign recognizing more than each other. Those ominous weeks, the silence since his departure had been discounted before they reached their table. As she first sat down, glancing his way without curiosity, pulling her gloves off slowly, she had rejoiced in this waste of moments; she was prodigal of security. In fact, she had waited so long that the narrow scope of this hour was immaterial.

What they said had been inconsecutive. His mother's figure crossed the screen of their talk. Janet asked, 'Why *were* you so angry?'

'You know that you know. Don't let's –'

'All right. Look, Edward: in ten minutes we'll both have to go. There's nothing to say, is there?'

'Too much to begin.'

'Once there was nothing, now there's too much – Is that because we've no future? Or is that why we've no future?'

'Let's go now,' said Edward.

'You aren't afraid, are you?'

'Janet, are you?'

'No more than if I were going to die – There isn't, is there?'

'Not?'

'Any future?'

'No. None.'

'I know.' But bending her head with that old movement she looked involuntarily into the palm of her hand as though he stood there.

3

Marise Gibson soon heard that Janet was in town, for Mrs Thirdman went straight from the club to her daughter's flat. Hoping, she said, just to catch Theodora . . . Theodora was out, which was perhaps fortunate; she did not like her relations to walk in without telephoning. 'In view,' as she said to Marise, 'of everything.'

The two had perfected a system of half-allusion – it is not difficult for women to live together – and rarely had to say anything more direct than 'What are we out of?' or 'You are looking like death today.'

Her daughter's friend, displacing some gramophone records, proofs and curious drawings, offered Mrs Thirdman an edge of the divan. Everything looked very low, for the cigarette-box you reached into the grate; the lamps were practically on the floor. But perhaps contrast was grateful to Marise and Theodora, who stood about so much. Still with an air of civilly concealing her amazement, Marise, very negligent, cool and imposing, made tea for the visitor. She groaned in the kitchenette.

'So nice up here, airy,' said Willa, breathless; there had been no lift. The flat was an attic; the windows, at floor-level, let in a draught round the feet and viewed some tree-tops.

'Yes, it's convenient,' said Marise, warming a little. 'Everything fits inside everything else; we had them designed, you know. We've had the mantelpieces taken away, so there's no dust. I hate a place where one cannot put things away, though one may never want to – I'm afraid this may be impossible tea, Mrs Thirdman. You see, we never drink any. You don't eat, do you?'

'No, that will be lovely, I'm sure,' said Willa, gratefully contemplating her cup – in which dust from the tea-leaves rose in a light film. The alarming girl supported herself against a bookcase.

'Do you know where Janet is staying? You see, Theodora will want to know. She can't be with Lady Elfrida as she's in Ireland. Besides, things are difficult just at present . . . You know?'

'*Won't* you keep me company?' said Willa, gesturing with the teapot.

'Thank you; I really would rather not. Perhaps Janet might like to come here, if nothing's arranged? She need not talk to us. As a matter of fact, we shall both be out tonight and we never speak in the mornings anyhow. But there's plenty of hot water, she could have baths and telephone.'

'I think there is always a little hotel she and Rodney –'

Willa could not feel that Janet would be quite at home in the flat. In a varnished colour-scheme of almost menacing restraint there were scimitar-curves and discs and soaring angles. She saw Janet more in that little hotel near St James's, where if last year's fog were never entirely polished off the brass knobs of the bed, the chintz was quite limp with prestige and the kind chambermaid who forgot the hot water remembered Rodney's grandfather.

Marise continued to contemplate, with alarming detachment, the little group Willa composed with the teatray and divan. 'I hear,' she said, 'that Edward is looking wretched.'

'Laurel only said he was feeling the heat.'

'But what a heredity!'

'Oh, I do hope not!' Willa rebalanced the tray, in great agitation. 'Janet did not get up in time to join us all at the club, so Edward was giving her lunch. It seemed so nice.'

'Really?' said Marise, without moving an eyelid.

'Sometimes, Laurel says, Edward has no time for lunch at all.'

'Did Laurel strike you –?'

'Look, I am taking still more of your delicious tea!' said Willa hastily.

'I'm afraid it is too repellent. I must say,' Marise went on, 'one can't help being sorry for Edward.' And lighting a cigarette she became lost in gloomy reflection. 'Did you hear,' she said suddenly, 'we've had a green china bath put in? It's square; the water runs in from the bottom; I must show you. It makes such a difference to life.... Of course, poor dear little Laurel is so diffusive.'

'I am devoted to Laurel,' said Willa warmly.

'Oh? Perhaps you're like me, no one really annoys me these days . . . Are you going? This is too sad.'

'I *musn't* take up any more of your time.'

'I hate work,' said Marise, accompanying her visitor to the top of the stairs. 'I would rather do anything. Theodora'll be sorry — you do know our telephone number, don't you?' she added gently.

'An interesting life,' thought Willa, descending the hair-pin flights. She felt the top of her head still exposed to a cool glare; perhaps only the skylights. An interesting life, she repeated. Yet twenty-six years ago she had borne Theodora — to what? For this? And an idea remained in her mind that the furniture in the flat was made of ground glass; the idea found its way into her talk and, distressing to Alex, had to be extirpated. Marise's manner was faultless; she had asked: 'How are your hollyhocks?' But not as if she had seen a hollyhock grow.

Willa, coming out into Buckingham Palace Road, looked longingly west towards Chelsea, reluctantly east to Victoria. An hour before the train was still on her hands, too short to drop in and see how Anna and Simon had grown, too long to spend in Gorringe's, even the Stores. She resigned herself to the hour's nonentity, boarded a No. 11 bus and was carried towards the terminus. She wished she had a married daughter in London, even a sister-in-law. She walked in St James's Park. 'Edward Tilney,' she thought, 'seems to be very much in the air just at present . . .'

But later, Alex made light of it.

In any case, Anna and Simon would not have been found at home in Royal Avenue. Their mother had sent them out with the cook, with a shilling each, to take tea under a coloured umbrella in Kensington Gardens.

'But we would rather go to the pictures.'

'Oh, *Anna*, this lovely day!'

'But the weather is always the same inside the pictures.'

Laurel knew she would weep, here, in the hall, with Sylvia watching. (The persistence of Sylvia in Laurel's life after so many years may appear remarkable. She had left, of course, shortly before Anna's birth, crossed the Park, occupied several situations in Bayswater, become a lady housekeeper, had a fine little boy by a commercial traveller and returned to Laurel a year ago, at very much higher wages and still more respectable.) It was half-past three and, composedly as a visitor, her sister Janet waited for Laurel upstairs. As in a dream, Laurel could not get to the drawing-room, where Janet waited. It was terrible. Sylvia, opening the hall door, let in some of the hot afternoon. The sun had gone off the front of the house; that was one mercy.

'Cheer up, Anna; we're going to Brittany.'

'I don't want to go to Brittany; I wish I had never been born.'

When Sylvia had got them both out and shut the door, Laurel said: 'So do I!' furious. Down the Avenue, she could picture the two of them lagging, angry, disconsolate, on their way to the 49 bus; Anna in the gay pink smock she had been given to wear at Batts, Simon with a panama in imitation of Considine's. Sylvia had orders not to return them before their bedtime. Then what did Mrs Tilney propose to do about dinner? 'We won't have any dinner; we'll dine out somewhere!' Of course, Edward would be furious.

Last year, she would have told him to look for another wife.

When Laurel did reach the drawing-room, where Janet sat in the high-backed chair by the empty grate, it was not, as one mistress of a house to another, necessary for Laurel to explain . . . In ten years, many of the wedding presents had been broken or put away. The room was sadder, civiller, less inconsequent, a room that ten years ago, with some tears and quarrels but all in a glow, had been contrived together and chatted about. Its order was now fixed; you must not move the furniture or a patch of ghostly new carpet appeared, that had not faded. The cupidy clock ticked on, a heart on its pendulum: Cousin Richard who had presented it was now Simon's godfather, safe in New Zealand. The shagreen cigarette-box was still in evidence.

'– Oh, it's empty, Janet; I'm so sorry.'

'I don't smoke, really.'

'No, but you did want to – Is the traffic too loud? Shall I shut the window?'

'The King's Road traffic?' said Janet, surprised. 'No, I hardly hear it.'

'You see how it is: there's never anywhere for the children to be when they're not anywhere special – Why do you look at me?'

'Was I looking? How?'

'You were – Oh, *what is the matter*!'

Janet could not begin to say; there was no measure for this. She felt strong and light, unlike herself, with a new spirit. She might be dead, for she could no longer be called to account. Dead, but not disembodied; there was a singular pleasure in feeling her right hand lie on her left, in looking down at the rose she wore, in being, in such a powerful stillness of body, bodily present here in this room with Edward written across it, among the restless evidences of his life.

Laurel saw Janet would not understand. Her tone changed; she said: 'But how good you were to come up!'

'I had to, of course I wanted –' Janet began. She broke off and went over to Laurel to comfort her. 'Don't, *don't*,' she cried, all consternation and pity. She could not see Laurel's face, which was against her shoulder; she was mistaken, Laurel was not weeping. A shiver, as at some terrifying awakening, passed for a sob. Wide open, Laurel's unseen eyes, unseeing, were dark and steady with incredulity. Relaxing her body she gave herself up to Janet's consolation idly, as though to a child's. Her head dropped, her hand made a fumbling, afflicted movement on Janet's shoulder. She let consternation flow through her out into a void. In the room, life all centred in Janet, in her passionate fatality. For minutes this travesty of consolation continued.

'Laurel . . .'

'I wish we could just go back.'

'To being no one but you and I?'

'Is that what you'd like?' said Laurel, with desolate incuriosity.

'I don't know; I can't remember.'

'*Answer* – no, don't answer. What is the good?'

'We have never asked each other –'

'There never was anything – What a long time you've waited, Janet. You've waited, haven't you? And how well Elfrida knew. She's always been seeing something over my shoulder; she's been my most frightful enemy. No wonder Edward was restless. Funny, I seemed to have everything, didn't I? And I've got no friends really but people like Mother and Willa and Mrs Bowles. I've never been anything but a daughter.'

'I wish you'd be angry –'

'Have I seemed very ridiculous all these years? I thought I was doing so well. What a wedding day, what rain, what a frightful mistake! But no one could tell me.'

Janet realized she had been holding Laurel too long, that any life in the touch had departed; she went back to her chair. The catastrophe was very quiet.

'When did you know?' she said.

'When that-fool Theodora wrote. First it seemed all silly, but rather exciting; like the beginning of a war. It never struck me not to give Edward the letter. Then I saw he, I saw Edward – It was much more than just his mother. I remembered how you and he quarrelled when you were engaged to Rodney: I saw why I minded so much then. Edward and I never quarrel; we fight. Before he went off to Batts, I said what I'd never dared say, what I'd never even thought: "There's no reason why you *should* keep minding so much about Elfrida!" '

'He really did mind, Laurel.'

'Oh, he didn't – How curious, Janet; you don't know him! But he had to have something to live on.'

'You're saying more than you mean.'

'I didn't mind seeing: I love him so much; I do love him. But this idea of Elfrida, what she had, what she was, has been fearful; it's ruined us all. We've been certain of missing something, we've all watched the others. Like that game, a ring going round and round on a circle of string under everyone's hands – you never know where it is, who may have it. It's been terrible, Janet, it has, it has really. It's ruined us all.'

4

At this inadmissible crisis Lady Elfrida was elsewhere, the Irish side of the Channel, innocently abroad. Edward, that same day, left Whitehall early for home; but, unwilling to arrive, regretted a no-destination: his mother's shut-up house with paper over the carpets and sheeted furniture. In St James's Park, rounding the lake with its screaming water-fowl under the heavy July trees, he recollected a quality in her welcome and that something in her affection, a touch of cheerful ignorance. For a hundred omissions to smile when her smile overruled him, he craved pardon. She was away. For the moment, London was simply a shell to him, stamped with her absence. Could she ever have missed him? Besides some small marks for her irony, he had offered her little enough.

There was, all at once, nowhere for Edward to go; he felt too old for his world; he had graduated.

Since Trevor Square was not in existence, he did not doubt that Janet would be returning that day to Batts. She had not said so, she had said nothing; they had hastily parted. Her face with no look, a perfectly blank face after a smile, interposed between himself and his thought: he turned from it.

There was now nothing not to be done, but part or speak, which both were impossible. They would continue in their two customary directions, prosecuting existence. By this time, the shipping offices round Pall Mall would be closed: he should have called in to confirm the family bookings for St Malo. For some years, the Tilneys had been anxious to go abroad. They had desired solitude, unlimited time for talk, space, unorganized leisure. But summer after summer, inevitably, they had joined the Meggatts at Batts. Now that they stood committed to *villeggiatura*, a Brittany beach, could they swim, sleep, eat but not speak? Laugh but not touch? Touch but not look? Laurel made silence her enemy. But perhaps this was her reticence? He had never inquired.

By half-past six return became less impossible; Edward reached home. Laurel had bought those gay sprigged cotton dresses to take abroad. She was trying them on; she had added more than a touch of make-up – she said, to anticipate sunburn. Edward, seated on the stool by her dressing-table, watched her turn one pretty shoulder and then the other to the long looking-glass. Catching at his reflected half-smile, she quickly turned to him. Sylvia, she said, had taken the children to Kensington Gardens: he and she would have to dine out. – At the Queen's, perhaps?

He rather liked the idea. 'Let's ask Lewis.'

'I think he's dining with Janet: she's in town for the night, you know.' She named the hotel.

'Then let's ask somebody else.'

'Oh, Edward? Bother!'

'All right then, darling.'

'The fact is, Edward, I'm feeling a little bilious.'

'Then it seems a pity –'

'No, I'd like just a little dinner then come home early.'

'That's pretty,' said Edward, touching a frill of the pink dress.

'Not bad,' said Laurel, smiling at her reflection. Re-tying the fichu, she told herself that marriage was a good thing: she had no pride, it was a good thing he should be obliged to love her. Perhaps what she liked was proximity. For look how she had been missing Janet since four o'clock. She powdered her bare arms with orange powder and held them out. 'Sun,' she said.

In the glass, she saw Edward's eyes on the pink flounce, resolutely expressionless. To his reflection stole her long tender look that her looking-glass only received and perhaps recorded. Too shy to make herself known, she stood smiling in contemplation of her pretty feminine envelope; as though Edward were someone to whom she had already said good-bye, who had left her then slipped back for something forgotten; someone in haste, unwilling to be detained, impossible to accost, so that she must only secretly watch through the crack of a door or over the banisters his ghostly coming and going.

'What did I say?' said Edward, rousing himself.

'This day week we shall be in Brittany. Anna is furious. I suppose we do like her to have ideas of her own?'

So they dined at the Queen's, discussing Anna, who was a constant surprise to them and, in the incalculable variability of her mulishness, something of an achievement. Laurel finished her peach and said she felt better now but would like to go home. Edward said he would go for a turn. They said good-bye in Sloane Square; Edward put Laurel into a taxi. The night was stuffy; like needles a few stars pierced the density of the sky. Naturally, she did not ask . . .

Edward walked a short way up Sloane Street, then directed a taxi to Janet's hotel. Lewis, of course, would be with her. He had some idea that Lewis and he might walk home. He found the two looking through some manuscript under a high chandelier in a little sitting-room: a bright little dull room with console tables and gilt ferns climbing the mirrors.

'We are looking at Marise's novel.'

'Oh! Do you know about novels, Lewis?'

'No, I have no ideas. But Marise gave it to me.'

'We are thinking of something for Lewis to say,' smiled Janet.

Edward said he considered sending round novels in manuscript a form of exhibitionism, and invited Lewis to walk home with him. Janet sat dazzled under the light, putting the chapters in order; she said mechanically: 'Don't all go.' – By this time she had almost given up Edward, she had begun to think he would never come. She passed him the manuscript to put down somewhere, but did not look up. She wore dark red lace and looked at once more and less than herself; a country lady from home. Lewis declared it was hot, opened the window behind the lace curtains and went out to order Edward a drink. Immediately Janet's eyes met Edward's; she said: 'You must make him go.'

'I'll go away with him and come back.'

'No, that's – Very well: anything.'

Lewis did not lend himself to the subterfuge; he was determined to go without Edward. This idea of his own made him awkward, even abhorrent to both of them. It became plain to Janet, leaning back on the rigid sofa, her eyes shut, protesting she was tired, that she was assisting at some kind of murder. The degree was indifferent to her. Innocence, under repeated blows from them both, kept raising again and again a bloody head as Lewis, hat in the hand that waved off Edward, protesting unsociability, indisposition, a recollected engagement, kept backing towards the door. His look of candid sympathy, of affection, went from Janet to Edward. The sickening conflict ended; disingenuousness, hydra-headed, had many smiles. Edward went off with Lewis.

Janet, a moment later, went out to tell the porter not to admit Edward again, to tell him to tell Edward that she had gone to bed. But the porter was not there; Janet returned to the sitting-room. When Edward came back, she was on the sofa where he had left her. He shut the sitting-room door.

She said: 'Why couldn't we let him go naturally?'

'I thought you . . .'

Janet looked at her hands as though they were guilty. Her hands trembled.

'Is this your own room?'

'No. Isn't it ugly? But no one will come in.'

'Don't let's be angry now,' he said gently.

'No. Edward, do, do let us be quiet or something. Or come near me. Else why did you come back?'

The window, looped with lace, gave on an unlit courtyard: there were silent windows above, and below voices. Edward took Janet in his arms. He felt her face cold against his; her life unextended, deep in the compass of the moment, at a dark standstill and past astonishment.

The shock past, there had been no shock; they parted again in silence, Janet trembling. She did not let his hand go but kept feeling along his fingers with a light desperate touch as though she were blind. If she were less or more at peace, she gave no sign. She said at last: 'There is nowhere for us to be.'

'Now?'

'Ever. We've got nowhere.'

'This afternoon I thought . . .'

'Don't think; not yet. Oh, don't leave me.'

'We're mad, Janet – the window . . .'

'I know, I don't care. Let us for once not mind!'

'Oh, you beautiful . . .'

'No, go now,' she said, drawing away, trembling. 'Do go.'

'I haven't the strength,' he said. Her fingers paused on the back of his hand.

'I can't stay here without you. I can't live without you. I'll go home to Batts tonight.'

'You can't.'

'There's a one-o'clock train,' she said, her face held up, agonized to the light, finding words with difficulty. 'I shall be home sometime.'

'Good-bye?' said Edward.

She had to face the withdrawal of everything; her look went round his fixed look in a curious wounded way, lost. At a movement he made she smiled, as at something dear and familiar. She searched from feature to feature, learning the mask, almost unaware of him. While she exposed to his eyes her suddenly very young, perplexed, enlightened and very lovely face, he could feel her assemble, give out through her very wound itself some power, dark in the light she had from him, impalpable to the senses, impenetrable by the spirit. They still could not speak or part. His

133

will was not hers, nor hers his; their will like a frozen waterfall seemed to be timelessly standing still.

'Good-bye?' he asked again.

'Do we have to say that? Don't waste my courage at the very beginning.'

'Janet . . . ?'

'What am I saying? This is the end.'

'You don't know.'

'We made each other no promises.'

'You're right,' said Edward, very white. 'How could we?' he added with a kind of exalted bitterness. 'What are our promises worth?'

'As much as Elfrida's.'

'She –'

'Don't speak of her!' cried Janet; this first identity of their thoughts was horrible. 'She was her own; she spent her own life. But you and I –'

'We're less free?'

'No. I mean,' she said with a curious lift of the eyelids, a fixing of her distended pupils upon his own, 'we have no – no bitter necessity.'

'– Don't move, don't change: you're so beautiful. I never guessed what a woman was – If this must be the end, can't we once comfort each other?'

'No – I pray you not – I can never be touched again –'

Drawing apart, they both looked vaguely towards the door. Steps were crossing the corridor. They had in the moment of this retraction so utterly parted that they were lost to each other; each shut up in a confusion of aching senses. The footsteps halted and went away. Janet glanced round at the mirrors, at the prim attentive chairs like a world waiting.

'What is the time?'

'Twelve o'clock.'

'Oh,' she said, 'Wednesday.'

5

At Batts, Hermione paddled down the lake at a terrific speed, shrieked and leaped from the boat to the bank to take aim. 'Bang! Bang!' she exclaimed. She was pursued by a mad swimming buffalo.

'Now then, Hermione,' said her father from the top of the bank.

'I'm perfectly calm.'

'Anyhow, don't wake your mother.'

'She can't hear, right up there.' Hermione could not take her eyes from a spot in the lake where the buffalo sank in fury, in red ripples. 'Besides,' she added, 'she's isn't asleep, she's just been to the window.'

'But the curtains are drawn.'

'I know, she drew them.'

'Play some quieter game,' said Rodney. 'Fish.'

'Well, I can't at present: I'm a trapper.'

Rodney turned and went restlessly up the banks and lawns to the house. He had no time, he should be getting along. But the strangeness of Janet's early morning return, a strangeness that still hung over the scene, had communicated itself in all directions. At six that morning, she had telephoned for the car from Market Keaton. Perhaps now she could not sleep; there was some wind. The July trees, glossy, fretted the sky with their disturbance of light; standing under the house he could hear her stiff chintz curtains whisper against the window sill. In the bright midday with its slow hurry of clouds the house rather wearily stared, as though wearily seen. Stepping out of the car she had explained nothing, accounted for nothing; she had forgotten – forgotten, perhaps, to sleep.

She wanted to be at home, she said. But what unaccountable rashness, her all-night journey! Pitching his voice low, Rodney called up: 'Janet?'

Janet lay with her hands clasped under her head. She could not sleep, she was ashamed to be lying here. Ruled through her thought that was no thought, the unseen skyline behind those billowing curtains sustained the enormous day. She was the earth,

hooped round with roads and netted with railways, intolerable to
itself, afflicted by movement, nightless. From the train, sleepless,
not yet delivered from yesterday, she had watched this irresistible
new day dawn. On time she had some terrifying overdraft. Where
are they all, she thought; what can that be? – hearing a door shut.

Her door opened soundlessly; Rodney came in. On the draught,
to meet him, bright yellow day through the curtains made a wild
entrance. 'Rodney?'

'Not alseep?'

'No: I was going to get up.'

'Are you sure you're all right?' He sat down at the foot of the
bed. 'For Heaven's sake, Janet, don't do that again! No day is
worth it.'

She smiled. 'I know, Rodney.'

He looked at her, not quite like a doctor, more plainly puzzled.

'The Mothers' Union are coming today,' she added. 'The cakes
are made, but I've given no other orders.'

'I thought that was one thing you didn't belong to?'

'I ought. Anyhow, they're coming here for their Day. Can you
let me have Sykes and Benson to carry the trestles and benches
down from the loft?'

'I don't think the loft's a good place to keep them, do you?'

'I know; we must reorganize. This evening the men can cover
the tables and seats with tarpaulins and let them stay for the
League of Nations.'

'League of Nations?'

'Coming on Thursday.' In sudden search of darkness she put
her hands over her eyes.

'No, look here, Janet; you must stay where you are.'

'No, I must have those tables put in the right place.'

'If you're really *not* going to sleep, I'd like to hear about everything,' said Rodney wistfully. 'I'll just stay five minutes. You
seem to be hardly back yet. You did have a good day, didn't
you?'

He liked to be with her like this, she passive in the swaying light
from the curtains. Her feet were crossed in their scarlet mules;
for company he put a hand beside them. 'And so?' he said.

'Well, it turned out Laurel was giving Mother and Mrs Bowles
and Willa lunch at the club, so I had lunch with Edward. Then –'

'Where did you lunch? How was Edward?'

'The Ionides. Edward was quite well. Then I took a taxi to Laurel's and we –'

'How was Laurel? What had she done with your mother and Mrs Bowles?'

'Quite well – Oh, left them somewhere, I think. There was the usual fuss with Anna and Simon.'

'Surely it's time those two went away to school somewhere?'

'Laurel thinks it would ruin their characters. So then we talked –'

'Is she looking forward to Brittany?'

'Very much. So we talked: then Lewis rang me up.'

'How did he know you were there?'

'He had heard from Marise who'd heard from Willa who went round to look for Theodora after lunch. So he rang up and asked me to dine somewhere. Laurel couldn't have me because she'd sent the cook out with the children to Kensington Gardens; so I said I would. Then I went back to the hotel and had a bath, but when Lewis called for me I was still so tired I didn't want to go out; I asked him to stay and dine there.'

'I shouldn't have called that a very tiring day: didn't you shop? You generally do so much. What sort of a dinner did they give you?'

'The hotel? Oh, bad.'

'They always do. I can't think what made you –'

'So then we looked at Marise's novel.'

'Oh, can Marise write novels?' said Rodney, impressed. 'What was it about? Was it good?'

'Oh . . . women's difficulties, difficulties about women: I don't remember. I didn't think it seemed very good.'

'Did Lewis think it was good?' pursued Rodney.

'He didn't say. Then Edward came round to look for Lewis.'

'How did Edward know Lewis would be there?'

'You see, Lewis had rung up when I was at Laurel's – then after that Lewis and Edward walked home.'

'Good for Edward; he never gets enough exercise. So then you came home?'

'I was meaning to go to bed, but then I decided I wouldn't stay, after all. I remembered all this down here – the Mothers coming – and London was so stuffy; my room was so stuffy when I was dressing for dinner. So I decided to come home. Of course,

I had to pay for my room. But the midnight train was beautifully cool, Rodney. – Oh, yes, I know, I'm sorry: I've been an idiot. I won't do it again. Yesterday wasn't really a good day for me to go up.'

'But you did enjoy yourself?'

'Oh, yes; I'm glad I went.'

'What are you going to do with the Mothers' Union?'

'There's a treasure-hunt, and Hermione is going to take them out on the lake. I think perhaps, Rodney, I might sleep for half an hour.'

'I do wish you would. I say, Janet, it wasn't awkward with Edward in any way?'

'I don't understand,' she said, helplessly.

'The Elfrida business.'

'Oh, no; I think that has quite passed off.'

He kissed her.

'Dear Rodney . . .'

'I'm glad you're back,' he said, and crept out as though she were asleep already. Outside, his step quickened: this was a busy day for him. 'That was how it all was, you see,' said Janet aloud. She lay still, there were no more footsteps. Getting up, she looked out between the curtains. Hermione dragging a long flag over the grass, the lawn, the beeches . . . Had there been some mistake? Janet asked herself: 'What can Hermione be doing with that flag? It belongs to Colonel Gibbons; it ought to have gone back after the fête.' Hermione, tripping and tweaking like a sparrow, dragged at the yards of tri-colour bunting; the French flag writhed on the grass behind her.

Hermione was lining the punt with flags, for the Mothers: this soon became evident; she was up again from the lake for another flag. 'What ideas she does have,' thought Janet. Lying down again, she repeated, 'What ideas we all have; we do all have ideas. We do each other no good. Oh, my darling, we do each other no good.' In the lonely room, turning over, she pressed her cheek to the pillow.

Elfrida appeared to be giving Janet her diary which, she said, had never been written. 'There's a good deal you will not be able to read,' she added. 'You remember when you were in Paris –' Janet remembered when she had been in Paris. 'He went out.

Though he might be there again, I knew he would never come back.' Elfrida went away, dragging across the floor of the Ionides, over Laurel's carpet, the long French flag. The red-and-blue flowed and writhed; Janet could not prevent her. 'To decorate my life,' explained Elfrida.

Rodney would not have the mistress disturbed; she slept through lunch-time, into the afternoon. At three, it was Hermione who crept up to listen to the silence behind her door. But at half-past, with Rodney absent, having received no orders, the household rustled, coughed, tapped and at last broke in in consternation. This was without precedent. Her death only, which they more than half expected, would have appeased them. And so, indeed, she lay: no wind now, the room heavily quiet, the Tilney photographs staring along the mantelpiece.

If she pleased –? they said. The Mothers from the village were already arriving. She had not slept like this since the birth of Hermione. As she woke up, a baby wailed and voices came up from the lawn where in the deepening sunshine, among a few shadows, the Mothers were already assembling.

6

Laurel also had watched this Wednesday in. Cutting out the Chelsea roof-line, feeling about her bedroom with cold fingers, it made an extraordinary demand on her faith, her religion almost: a dependence upon the usual. Edward was still absent.

Past midnight, waking, startled by his smooth bed, going down in vain to call through the house where in room after room his absence made itself palpable, she had understood: Edward had not come in. She returned to her room. Such hours it is not desirable, not possible to record. First she found herself dreading each step, each taxi for its deception, then she longed for any step, any taxi for its very deception's sake, the stirring of hope. At half-past four – by the stroke of three clocks imperfectly synchronized, so that the moment was in itself protracted, deformed – Laurel ceased to expect him. By now there was daylight enough, the lamps ghostly, the street too plain – she turned from the window. After this no more clocks struck, something had died down somewhere or been arrested. She rang up the exchange to hear a voice, to be told the time. This verified the solidity of the hour. It was next day without him: such things happened.

Laurel dabbed her face with skin-tonic, ran a comb through her hair and went down again to the drawing-room. Here desolation gave her a curious lightness and liberty; she could have played patience or played the piano. She sat down, then took up an *Evening Standard* Edward had brought home. The telephone remained silent. It was clear she must not ring up anybody before seven.

She would not speak to Janet direct: at seven she rang up the hotel porter and asked him to have Janet waked and given a message. 'To come round to Royal Avenue as soon as she can.' The porter told her that Mrs Meggatt had given up her room and left about midnight.

'Oh, of course. Did she leave a message?'

'Mrs Meggatt left no message, madam.'

Was the porter concerned for her or was that sleep in his voice? Had she not sounded natural? 'Oh, yes, gone?' she should have said, 'of course; I remember.' She shivered. How much she had wept, all her life; how kind tears had been!

Anna, hearing her mother on the telephone, came downstairs in her pyjamas eating a piece of Genoa cake. The floor was in squares of early sunshine. Her mother, looking like a schoolgirl in her nightdress, sat on the sofa by the window, the *Evening Standard* spread out over her knees. She must be cold, she shivered; the newspaper rustled.

Annoyed, Anna said: 'Mother!'

'What are you doing with that cake?' her mother countered, mechanical.

'What one does do with cake,' said Anna calmly.

'Filling up your inside with currants at this hour.'

'I don't see it's worse than telephoning!'

'Oh, please, *please*, Anna!'

Anna had some sensibility. 'Your feet must be cold,' she said, 'bare and everything.' And without more ado she went up for Laurel's slippers. Laurel thought: 'What can I say?' – 'Bring down my dressing-gown too,' she shouted. The child, reappearing, asked: 'Where's Father? He hasn't slept here.'

'He's out.'

'How extraordinary. Why?' Anna wrapped Laurel up in the blue dressing-gown, then stood, with her square calm face so like Janet's, munching her Genoa cake and dropping crumbs on the floor. 'Why?' she repeated. Her mother did not reply. Anna had an immediate sense of emergency; she entertained several possibilities, all of them dire, without either relish or horror.

'What does Aunt Janet say?'

'Oh, but she's gone, you know, Anna.'

'But she was going to stay in London,' said Anna, aggrieved. 'Suppose we telephone Grannie.' (Mrs Studdart was 'Grannie'.)

'*No*,' Laurel said violently. Anna, having finished her cake, sat down on the sofa close to her mother and brushed some crumbs from her pyjamas, implying: 'Then we are deserted.' Laurel, feeling the warm young shoulder against her own, thought: 'What a comfort Anna would be to anyone else.' But love, with any faculty for relationship, had quite gone out of her. Anna suddenly asked: 'You are speaking the truth, aren't you?' Drawing sharply away, scarlet, she said: '*Has he been arrested?*'

Laurel kept this for Edward, a key to Anna.

Then it was simply, Anna could see, that he had deserted them, taking away the tickets to France. She had heard of things of this kind, in Sylvia's talk. She rejected her father, closing herself to him in every direction – the cool pleasure she took in his charm, his looks; her appreciation of his propriety; the countenance she gave to his pranks, to his versatility. For hours she had, for love, fatigued herself to amuse him, played hot, dishevelling games with him: pirates and so on. But now, he – her mind stretched tip-toeing up for some final fatal word – he is impossible. Then her mind ran down to the kitchen, to join their talk. It's that Elfrida – they are a lot, they are! Not real fathers or grandmothers, not respectable. Mother has no idea. Now the Studdarts have always been respectable. Let us go back to Cheltenham. Let Uncle Rodney adopt us: we should never have come away. Aloud, she said to her mother: 'I expect what you want is a nice cup of tea.'

'– Anna, would you say I was stupid?'

'If I was you,' said the child, 'I should have a good cry – And do come away from the window, there is the milkman.'

It was Lewis, if anyone, that Laurel ought to consult. He was the prepared surface, utterly confidential. Lewis, however, she

141

would at all costs avoid. The morning rose like a flood isolating mother and daughter, with its wide view of desolation. Simon, who had escaped his bath, hung about saying: 'What shall I do?' (Anna would tell him nothing.) 'Some day,' said his mother, 'I'll teach you to play patience.'

'Mother, when can I buy that gimlet to take to France?'

About ten o'clock, while Laurel was in the kitchen (if the servants had even ever-liked Edward it would not have been so difficult, but Sylvia had seen two homes broken up, there was nothing she did not know about gentlemen; it was unfortunate she had ever come back), Anna crept to the telephone in the drawing-room and on her own initiative rang up Lewis. ('He was telephoned for late last night, it was most urgent,' Laurel maintained, below-stairs, to heavy suspicious faces,)

Anna asked Lewis if he thought it likely her father had been run over. Lewis was at pains to collect himself; for a moment he hoped this was some savage joke of which Anna might well be capable.

'I don't think that would happen, do you?' Anna continued. 'He's so very careful. Do you think we ought to advertise? Or do you know of any good police station?'

'What does Aunt Janet advise?'

'Oh, she's gone off, too,' said Anna impatiently.

'What *do* you mean, Anna?'

'She went off in the middle of the night.'

'How do you mean, gone off?' cried Lewis in great agitation. 'Do you mean she's gone home?'

'I've no idea,' said Anna, indifferent. 'The thing *is*, Mr Gibson . . .'

'Have you telephoned to Batts?'

'Mother won't; she won't let me telephone to you, she won't let me do anything. I think what she needs is a good lie down . . . No, she won't do *that* on any account, either. I think she feels rather shy. As I say to her . . .'

'Yes, but she should get in touch with Rodney . . .'

'Perhaps if you did . . .'

But at this point there was a break. Laurel had come in (wearing the pink cotton frock she had bought for Brittany – it *must* be all right; look at her pink cotton frock!). 'What are you doing? How dare you!' she said. There was a scuffle, she snatched the receiver from Anna. 'Who's there, who's Anna talking to?' she exclaimed.

'It's Lewis,' said Lewis guiltily.

'Oh, Lewis . . . I expect there's been some mistake. I wish Anna hadn't –'

'But look here, Laurel, you must do *something*. You can't just wait there. You must get in touch with Rodney.'

'Why Rodney? I don't want to bother Janet.'

'But is Janet – ?'

'Can't you *see* it's impossible? There must have been some mistake; I didn't get some message.'

'What do you mean, impossible?'

'Nothing. I said *nothing*, Lewis . . . You saw Edward last night, didn't you?'

'Yes, we said good night at about eleven at the corner of Buckingham Gate. He said he was going to walk home. We had walked from the hotel.'

'Hotel?'

'Yes, Janet's hotel.'

A silence. 'Oh, yes, of course.'

'Janet seemed rather tired. I'd no idea she –'

'Yes, she's gone home, you know. She went last night.'

'I didn't know there was a train.'

'Well, there must have been, mustn't there, or she would not have gone.'

'Of course. But, Laurel, you must let her know; it's not fair to her. She'd send for you if –'

'I tell you: *no*, Lewis. Are you there? Can you *hear* me? I tell you, no! This is my affair, you've got to let me decide –'

'Look here, Laurel, let me come round.'

'No, thank you, Lewis . . . I'm so sorry Anna bothered you.'

'Have you rung up his department?'

'Yes . . . He wasn't there yet, but – Oh, there's bound to be some message.'

'Meanwhile,' said Lewis, 'I shall at least –'

'No, I'd rather you didn't. Please, Lewis,' she finished sharply.

She rang off. Her voice, sounding brittle, had splintered finally. Lewis thought: 'This has never happened before: there *is* no way to proceed. Now if he were only dead there'd be some formula . . .'

Lewis had seen Edward stop a taxi, seen the taxi swoop in the empty street and turn back to St James's.

This was wretched. Discomfort to Lewis, an almost physical irritation, some itch or tightness about the skin, a clamminess in the hands. He got up, a shocked little man starting up with a cry still conciliatory; protest yelled to the dam bulging, cracking above. 'No, look here, don't! You mustn't do that! Stop!' He met this catastrophic torrent like death with his vexation: small cup held up bravely to overflow with the first drops. Fear, anger, pride: these you dash to pieces empty: Death, these are me, they shall not contain you: they could not contain you!

So Lewis, aggrieved, staring out of the window, rejected the summer morning, light fresh on high flanks of the houses. He had a pang too, but less than a pang, for the wretched lovers.

Hating himself, and in direct contravention of Laurel's desire, Lewis presently went round to the hotel. Edward (well known here) had, he heard from the porter, returned soon after eleven and left again about midnight. Janet had given up her room, had her things brought down, paid her bill and left about half-past twelve, just as a theatre party came in calling for drinks. Owing to this disturbance the porter could not recall what directions she gave him to give the taxi. Otherwise, Mrs Meggatt had mentioned no destination. She wore day clothes, a dark wrap coat, looked and spoke as usual. A lady had rung up very early this morning, asking for Mrs Meggatt; a second lady, annoyed, had rung up an hour later. The porter respectfully hoped there was nothing wrong? He knew Lewis and seemed surprised by his manner. They both knew the same Mrs Meggatt.

'Mrs Meggatt has been called home,' said Lewis hurriedly: 'I just wanted to know she got off all right and – oh, to see that any letters are forwarded.'

There was a letter from Rodney for Janet.

'Nothing serious, sir, I hope?' said the porter with unction. It was clear he still did not care for Lewis's manner. 'How badly I do this: they should have had different friends.' It struck him that a decision of this kind, after ten or more years, would be arrived at quickly, calmly. Much discounted itself, after all, as a letter, they say, long unanswered answers itself. There would be brief or no consultation, his nervous efficiency, her common sense. Still the snug hall with red-carpeted staircase offered itself as the scene of piteous and futile departure: their love was homeless.

'Are we,' wondered Lewis – stepping out over the springy mat, standing still in the mounting glare of the street: a retired street with very white doorsteps and polished windows – 'to act, or not act? They've got their cue, but they're leaving all of us none.' Apart from this axiomatic selfishness of all lovers, Lewis told himself, Edward had been inconceivably heartlessly rude. He was never direct till now, thought Lewis angrily. He had moved in a haze of equivocations, all considered, all passably honourable. His charmingly adolescent reserve in love, his kindergarten paternity. – One would have said, at worst, your polite murderer. The violence of this departure, this outgoing from the self, appalled Lewis. A portrait had crashed down leaving, worse than a blank of wall, a profound recess in which there might or might not be eyes.

From Laurel there would be always the same cry, in despair, in wild resolution: 'Save them for me!' While her house fell like Usher's cracked through the heart, through the hearth; with where there had been fires the stare of a cold unsuspected moon: 'Oh, save them!' – honesty, nonsense, wit, all the dear conventions, happy custom.

When Lewis came in, Theodora was in his rooms. 'So –?' she said, preparing to be intolerable. They were both truculent. 'Well?' said Lewis. She had been there some time; he tipped a fuming ash-tray into the grate and brushed some ash from his table.

'Well what?' countered Theodora. 'As you weren't answering your telephone I came round,' she added.

'So I see.'

'What ought we to do?'

'I see no reason why we should do anything.'

'What about Rodney?'

'For God's sake leave Rodney alone,' said Lewis, violently.

There was a quite remarkable drop in her manner. 'So they *have* gone, really?' she said. For the first time, she had bluffed without pleasure. 'What a fool you are, Lewis,' she added drearily, 'how on earth could you think I knew? It was pure speculation – nightmare. They told me Janet had gone – we were to have lunched this morning; I rang her up. Then I tried to get Laurel;

when she heard me she fled and sent Anna to do the idiot child. And no one ever knew *you* be out at this hour! – Don't make faces, Lewis! – Of course,' she went on, unpleasantly, 'we know this is hard on you. So much to be arranged, so much popping in and out, such tact –'

'Whereas you enjoy this kind of thing.'

'Naturally,' said Theodora. Dramatic in her sincere misery, she stood biting her lip like a stage villain.

'Of course, they'll turn up again.'

'In which case it will be all right,' said Theodora.

'Really, we can't go into that – A drink, Theodora?'

'No thank you, Lewis.'

'Then perhaps if you don't mind –'

'Oh hell! oh hell!' said Theodora, rhetorical.

'Yes, I know. But you really must go if you're going to have hysterics.'

'I can't stand this; I love her! I tell you, idiot, I love her beyond propriety –'

Lewis wondered how he and Theodora had come to know each other so long without bloodshed. 'Yes, it is most upsetting,' he said icily. 'And never, never think of anyone but yourself. It would be fatal, wouldn't it, Theodora? I should go home and lie down.'

She really was unhappy. And what a good thing, thought Lewis, viewing the entire collapse of any charm she ever had, that she was not unhappy more often. 'I suppose,' he thought, 'they do really suffer.' She was so entirely to pieces that Lewis – by picking up again and handing to her her gloves and her cigarette-case as fast as she put them down again – had no difficulty in edging her from the flat.

'The fact is,' he admitted, taking a last shocked look at her through the bars of the lift, 'Theodora's jealous – And don't *talk*!' he shouted, as she began to descend. 'And don't bother Laurel.' He caught a last black look at his feet as her face passed them. She was furious, too. Such a moment for anger – impure, selfish fire. What *had* brought her round? Had their going scribbled itself across the sky of London? So savage rumour creeps through the forest, faster than any runner. Shaken, Lewis poured himself out a drink, though it was still so early. Yes, they were less than twelve hours upon their way.

146

Was this as Lady Elfrida expected? Her due, he thought
vaguely.

He drank without pleasure, leaning against the mantelpiece.
What had stung him to the personal quick? Was he chagrined,
or perhaps humiliated? Were those two by now out at sea, past
the buoys, on an ocean to unhappy knowledge not trackless but
scored bewilderingly? Land-bound, he hated their damned ship,
all damned ships, and hated those everlasting departures. 'We
all seemed to be getting along so nicely,' thought Lewis.

Watching a ship draw out you are aboard a moment, seeing
with those eyes: eyes that you can no longer perceive. You see
the shore recessive, withdrawing itself from you; the familiar
town; the docks with yourself standing; figures – but later (where
was the crowd?) all gone. The high harbour crane is dwarfed by
spires behind; there are buildings very distinct, paste-board
houses: you can still count the windows. Indifferently, you perceive some unknown relation, the hill right over the church –
lovely, the light church backed by the dark hill: you often went in
without looking up. The opera house and the station are brothers,
with twin arcades. The steep avenue to the observatory you never
mounted – now the whole town is ruled by that grave bubble. The
climbing terraces are in order, lending each other grace. You
look – as this all retreats – with regret but without desire. The
figures in trouble are inconceivable, gone. Your tear perhaps is
for some fine house with a portico, unknown, always to be unknown.

– So you looked back with those aboard, for a moment only.
So they depart; traitors to you, with you, in the senses. The ship,
those eyes, are for you ashore now inconceivable, gone. Under
the very high crane a winch creaks, clocks strike from the dwarfed
spires behind. The church hides the hill, terrace blocks out
terrace. The crowd that you are breaks up, looks out no longer,
recognizes futility. You all stand apart but still return to the town
two and three abreast in a kind of familiarity. There is some
awkward gesture, a word or two between strangers, a handker-
chief put away. But now, you all part; the ship is forgotten. So
you relinquish the travellers, the ship vanishes. That last exchange,
that identity of a moment, has taken everything; you have lost
even regret. The close town receives you in its confusion.

Lewis put down his empty glass on the mantelpiece, resolving

147

to see Laurel. She must not stay there alone. Besides, there must be something that she should do. Plans to make, possibly; or perhaps she should write letters.

7

Lady Elfrida did not leave a caretaker at Trevor Square. Nothing there would lock – she had few keys, actually: she mistrusted a caretaker's ennui and did not like to think of one roving about her house. So she left one latch-key with Edward, in case she wanted anything sent after her – he carried the key on his ring, with others – and arranged for a Mrs Thomson, her charwoman, to look in daily, open windows, dust if she cared, forward letters and report if anybody had broken in. For some weeks Mrs Thomson's visits were uneventful, but this Wednesday she had 'quite a turn'. Drawing up the drawing-room blinds, she discovered Mr Edward Tilney asleep on the sofa. The poor young gentleman – for so he still appeared – had taken off his shoes, pulled back the dust-sheet and now lay sound asleep with an air of great discomfort and restlessness, like a traveller who did not expect to sleep at all. Mrs Thomson screamed. He, opening his eyes without a sound, looked fixedly, calmly at her as though she were quite in order. He could not be himself at all. But he explained, as pleasantly as you could wish, that he had lost his own key, got locked out of his own house, and recollecting that he carried the key of his mother's, turned in here for the night. He hoped he had not alarmed Mrs Thomson? Mrs Thomson confessed that he had alarmed her and said she was only glad he had not been taken up. The constable on the beat was giving an eye to the house, she said. Edward told her he had avoided the constable. 'I should make a good burglar,' he added pleasantly. He sat up on the sofa rubbing his chin with a finger, looked with an odd air of recollection about the dismantled drawing-room and asked what time it was. She was pleased to tell him it was eleven o'clock – she expected there might be trouble somewhere for Mr Tilney. His poor young lady! However, he did not smell of drink – on this point it would have been impossible to deceive Mrs Thomson. He shut his eyes again for a moment, then got up and put on his shoes. She offered him a cup of tea; he said he felt more like a shave and a clean collar; he must go out for both. Mrs Thomson, who had sons of her own, was sorry later she had not insisted on that cup of tea. From the balcony window, she saw him stop dead, oddly, half-way down Trevor Square.

He stopped dead, in the sun by the palings, but finding he could not think was alarmed and went on downhill, quickly, towards Harrod's. Harrod's should have a collar; would they also shave him? Laurel lay lightly on the surface of his mind, a skeleton leaf too frail to disturb water. His silence, his cruelty to her were transparencies, casting no shadow. Morning, Knightsbridge, the brown dome of Harrod's, Mrs Thomson's surprise: all weighed a little but nothing appeared extraordinary. He could never bear Laurel to be even a little troubled; now, supposing her desperate, he knew himself unchanged. There was no longer any impossible. He supposed he must now be delivered from something, free: this term with no bounds, incapable of appreciation, of measurement, spun in his head as he approached Brompton Road for his collar. He felt familiar with himself, heard his own step, looked down at his shadow.

This shadow of his on aching July pavements (for he was still very tired) he would not see now for long. They would be in France – he jumped the narrow but very deep interval to the week's end – in Brittany. He carried the tickets with him – here they were, all the time. On Saturday the Tilneys would shut up their London house and make their cheerful departure.

A query – the scarlet telephone-box ahead – made him contract. Telephone? He looked through the scarlet lattice: empty: the directory dangled. Telephone? He asked himself what any other man would have said to Laurel. But there was no other man. 'I could not come back to you. If I could have told you I could not, I could have come.' Quickening his pace, he passed the telephone; to pause farther down at a corner. Brompton Road roared, very close. As though his cruelty to her were something he had knowingly executed but not knowingly designed, something composed phrase by phrase, carved detail by detail or minutely painted standing close to the canvas, he had to stand back from it now with a new-comer's awe at its largeness, its ignorant boldness, its realization of some giant and foreign self in him.

The slow white passage east of some clouds, a stir here and there

149

in a high-up awning, suggested, above and round London, some warm disturbing wind. He supposed that at Batts, where Janet was now at home, wind would set up in that house built for calm – frosted mornings when trees were like images on the window-pane, immovable mists from the lake, the heaviness of late summer – some unrest, a strangeness to its own nature or, between the intermittent movement of curtains and shadows, a kind of tension. Or could she sleep through today? The dear monotony of her life, rising, covered what was to him her drowning face. Oblivion of her, of her whole look and her last look, had established itself in sleep with him; become, if he were indeed entombed, entombed here with him; become the intimate of his spirit. Became his very spirit itself that travelled about his cloudy idea of her form like a blind hand, without regret or desire. If he was to see her again he would see her familiarly downcast, looking nowhere, preoccupied. Her absences, her silences, her abstentions were now again informed by the only sense he had of her. If indeed between today and yesterday they had met, they had met unwilling; or else, too willing, had not met. Or perhaps last night after the whole day's feverish half-obscurity, the obscurity of the years, they had for the first time, enlightened, parted.

He thought of his wife. Dismissing her nearness to him in the spaceless present, the agonizing tension between them now of a silent telephone-wire, he saw her in flickering little sequences of their intimacy; Laurel putting all the Dresden china away – Oh, she cried, how had they ever lived with it! – trying on inscrutability, spinning a cushion to him across the floor, patting cream on her face from the chin up.

'I knew there would be a message,' she said to Lewis excitedly. 'I knew there had been some mistake! But thank you, Lewis, thank you so much! But I wish now we had never –'

She would have liked to offer Lewis lunch, but would have liked far better to see him go. Besides, there would be no lunch; she had not ordered any. There he still stood in the hall, looking at her askance: something must still be owing. It was half-past twelve; Edward's telegram had just now been delivered. Sandwiches – as though he had helped her put out a fire, as though they were moving house? She had not quite the heart for this. Dear Lewis – but how imperceptive he was! Would he never leave her? –

Anna was there in the hall with them, quite the grown girl, her arm through her mother's; very much present. Laurel could read in Lewis's manner – in so far as, having hardly assembled himself, he had a manner at all – that he thought it a pity Anna was not brought up like Hermione. He would have liked to ask her to run away. Laurel of course wished strongly to reassert the normal, but it would not be normal to ask Anna to run away. This was not Batts, Laurel was not Janet; there was nowhere for Anna to run to.

'All the same, I *don't* think so,' said Lewis, after an interval.

'Don't think what?'

'That we've made any unnecessary fuss.'

'Oh, all right, Lewis – Don't let's all stand in the hall.'

Of course, too many people were always present: at this very moment she heard Sylvia beginning to come cautiously up the basement stairs. 'I'm so thankful,' Laurel said, 'that Elfrida's in Ireland.'

'I don't see –' began Anna. This child who, having suddenly reinherited her whole life as Edward's daughter, stared so knowingly from beside Laurel's shoulder, certainly did antagonize Lewis. And someone ought to do something at once about Theodora, somebody ought to stop her . . . 'You were *mad*,' they ought to tell Theodora: one ought to bully her. Lewis and Theodora must meet forthwith. For her mind, with his own, was now the sole but still direful theatre of this large non-occurrence. Janet was home, asleep – Rodney had telephoned – Edward would soon be returning. The ship had not sailed, the aloe had not flowered.

'I don't see,' said Anna, '*how* he had breakfast at Trevor Square?'

'Let's go up to the drawing-room.'

'No – Look here, Laurel; I must be going.'

'Do stay, do have lunch!'

Laurel's bravado had reached a climax. She was quite wild; she had courage to waste, more now than she needed; she was quite overtopping the dreadful day. She laughed, was too natural, gaily manacled Anna's wrist as the child pulled away. For the child, overlooked, was once more furious with suspicion. They all knew her father had not breakfasted: something was still the matter; she was not being fairly used.

'You don't *seem* very glad!' she cried, and had to be appeased by them both – was she only Anna? She would feed on this morning, making her strong young growth, like a tree, from the very thought of ruin. But no; she knew nothing, they could be quite certain; she could guess at nothing of what had not occurred. Lewis and Laurel could not do enough to propitiate the little girl. She should go to the pictures without Simon: she should be given a parasol to take to France.

Lewis said he must really go. Laurel said good-bye at the foot of the stairs and was half-way up – so much of the day still claimed her – before he had opened the hall door. Then she turned anxiously, pushed past Anna, ran down to catch him. She said something rapidly about France, their departure, their holiday; good-bye now for some weeks, perhaps? '*So, Lewis* ...' She stopped, so urgently: that was all. He let himself out (there she still stood) and, shutting the hall door heavily, excluded himself and the street where on trees and railings a cloud moving east shed a bright, transient shadow. He had heard what she had not attempted to say: 'So please, forget ...'

That evening, Laurel comforted Edward. Not enough could be done to that end; he had suffered through her; she had had no idea of her power. He was so tired – how far had he walked? He guessed at some streets and squares and remembered the empty curve of Regent Street. Night had been cruel to him, so undefended; she could not bear to think of him homeless that whole hard night. 'If I could have been with you – I could have been anybody; I need not have been me.'

'But I did sleep, you know.'

'On Elfrida's sofa? It's so short.'

'The beds were all covered with newspaper; I touched one and it crackled. Besides, I found I didn't want to stay upstairs. You know that's always been like a strange house. All her things were about, not put away. I don't think she cares for them much, do you? She hardly lives there; this time she seemed to be gone for good. So I stayed in the drawing-room.'

'– The telephone's there –' But ashamed, she had hidden her face on his arm.

'I know; I looked at it.'

'I didn't *mean* to say that! Forgive me, I never – don't, *don't*,

Edward! Don't you see I'm so happy now? Don't let us ever —
Besides, I might not have heard. I was asleep too, you know, part
of the night . . . Why don't I know Elfrida? I've been dreadful
about her; I've sometimes wished she was dead. Did you know?
I'd have wished she'd never been born, only there had to be you.
Why can I not know her? Do you think she ever misses us?'

'But listen, Laurel —'

'Oh, do you have to tell me? Do you *want* to tell me?'

'Don't you want to know?'

'I know you're here again now.'

They talked, but not very much, by the drawing-room window
in the hot, retarded dusk; all the doors and windows stood open
to let air through the house which seemed to be empty, silent
below and above them. He remembered, she had not let him turn
up that playing-card on the floor on their wedding-day. He still
saw the pattern on the back of the card. She remembered nothing;
it was impossible to speak of forgiveness; that meant nothing,
nothing. She was so happy, she said again. Once or twice she
silenced him with her fingers or lips or in his arms drew closer
round them a darkness in which they had never needed to speak
of happiness. There was no question even of pity; this ruled that
out. Then drawing gently away herself, not her gentleness, leaning
her head on the window frame, she watched the roofs disappear
once more into the night. It had been a long day. She thought of
sleep and of a hundred solitary woman's wakings, beside but
without him; here, in their high room at Batts, or soon in that unknown room in Brittany within sound of the sea.

He said: 'It's late, isn't it?'

They had only to listen; three clocks struck, imperfectly
synchronized, deepening the moment.

'Simon's been marking off days on his calendar till we go to
France. How lovely; we're going away on Saturday!'

'Day after tomorrow.'

'Is it tomorrow now?'

He was right; it was almost tomorrow. All this time they had
been carried along on the smooth stream; they had only to keep
still, not rocking their boat.

8

At Corunna Lodge, Colonel Studdart's days were spaced out carefully, without intervals for perplexity. Mrs Studdart's were, on the
contrary, seldom ideal in size or shape; usually it was at least half
an hour later than she could have wished. She had become, she
said, her own daughter; typed diligently on Janet's machine,
walked the dog to the post before tea and drove the car into
Cheltenham. The couple went out to bridge, entertained at the
tennis club and enjoyed, one way and another, a good deal of
quiet society. Perhaps the garden, lately, suffered a little: she
dreaded sciatica, he did not care to garden for long alone. Two of
their poplars came down in the storm the year Simon was born;
the *prunus japonica* commemorating Hermione reached to the
height of the gatepost and branched extravagantly, but never to
the height of the porch repainted the year of the two weddings.
They did not miss their daughters but they regretted them. After
dinner, pulling round arm-chairs to the fire with backs to the
empty room, she played patience, the board over her knee; he
finished a detective story a night. If he died first, she would stay
on here for the grandchildren; if she died first the house would be
given up. Once or twice in an evening their eyes met.

They were fortunate in their sons-in-law. Rodney gave not a
moment's anxiety; on the other hand it was always possible for
Mrs Studdart to organize Edward a little. Besides an interchange
of family visits each daughter, disengaging herself from all newer
ties, returned solitary as a maid to Corunna Lodge once a year, at
one time or another.

Generally, Janet came in the early autumn. This cherished
wife of Rodney's was not uprooted easily from her soil: she
brought Batts in with her from the moment her dressing-case had
been carried upstairs. The shell-backed, gold-mounted brushes
and mirrors, the gold-stoppered bottles, the photographs in their
folding frames, the shagreen clock for her bedside, the rugs and the
cushions without which she was not allowed to depart – all set up
in the bow-windowed spare-room a minor establishment. The
journey had not been carelessly undertaken; her arrival became a
grave offering to their love. In return, the distractions of Chelten-

ham were, the parents observed with delight, delightful to their visiting daughter who lived such a quiet life. Therefore they gave little dinners, took her from house to house, attended concerts, the theatre. Still with her air of tranquil apartness, of having – and these they could not enough respect – attachments elsewhere, she re-entered the life of Corunna Lodge. She was consulted as to the redecoration of the morning-room. The photographs, the anecdotes, the reminiscences came out again for her yearly; she smiled or pondered. She brought her embroidery frame and, sitting on the window-seat in the mornings, the fender-stool at nights, discussed Hermione, Anna, Simon, Edward, dear Willa, queer Theodora, sympathetic Lewis and kind Mrs Bowles. Her mother led the talk, but Janet withheld no opinion that could be agreeable. She walked with her father – at Batts, alas, she said, one did not walk enough. She balanced Bordighera against Alassio and agreed that it would not have been well to have undertaken the journey to Madeira even could one have afforded it. Colonel Studdart asked what Considine really *did* do with himself: alas, she replied, too little. 'There are fellows even here,' said Colonel Studdart, 'who find days too long.'

It surprised the Studdarts to remember that they had not expected Janet to marry. She was the born married daughter. In youth, they remembered, she had been – though so good – unapproachable: one never knew what she thought. There were still, it is true, moments when Mrs Studdart became aware another woman was present; or felt constrained, perhaps, by this constant company in which her own daughter Janet, Rodney's wife or Hermione's mother remained impossible to discuss. While, once or twice, Colonel Studdart perceived a stranger. Surprising her in a room, or looking up at her from his book – some darkness or turn of the head, an arm crossing the light, a shadow displaced, a dress moving; he had a sigh, a pang, perplexity; here something forgotten stirred – a beautiful woman. He remarked to his wife how Janet's looks had improved. Though contented on her behalf they would have liked her to shine more widely, and sometimes thought vaguely of diplomatic dinner-parties.

Laurel Tilney's coming occasioned far more disturbance. She liked to sleep in her old room, from which tin boxes of Colonel Studdart's uniforms had therefore to be removed. But then she spread her dresses over the spare-room bed, so that she occupied two rooms, in point of fact. She came with her less imposing luggage for shorter visits; for though her establishment was not large her husband was sensitive. Also, there were the children to be arranged for; *they* had no Swiss maid: she had to send them across the Park to stay with Mrs Bowles. Her silver trousseau hairbrushes had dints in their backs. 'As though,' she said, 'Edward had been beating me.' Laurel drove the car through Cheltenham at immoderate speed and raced the dog to the post. Cheltenham was the country to her after London; she stepped in and out through the windows, hung up the old hammock and often began to mow the lawn. 'Your eye is still crooked,' said Colonel Studdart. Her arm was often through his; as of old, she kept pressing into his shoulder her sharp chin. She and her mother so frequently met in London that though she had less to tell than Janet there was for some reason more to say: nothing she began to tell them was ever finished; she was the old undirected talker. She still shook hands too vigorously; she went upstairs two at a time. Mrs Studdart said: 'Do you go upstairs like that in London?' 'Mother, I've no idea how I go upstairs in London. Do notice next time!' She still tore out photographs of good-looking men from the illustrated weeklies and, for lack of anything else to do with them, sent them to Edward.

Her old room, her white-painted bed should have seemed very narrow. Once or twice Mrs Studdart looked in, very late, to find Laurel curled up on her side, staring at the shell-shadow the electric light shade always cast on the ceiling. She could fall asleep from this; light had never affected her. 'Poor Edward's light bill must be tremendous,' said Mrs Studdart, darkening the room severely. In the darkness there was a movement, as though Laurel held her arms out, as though she were nine years old. Her mother continued: 'Does Anna stare at the light?'

'Anna?'

Yes, her coming again and again occasioned disturbance; it was like a birth in the house. She affected the very clocks; nothing seemed quite in order. She was there, brilliant, like sun that discovers a picture at five o'clock for a few days only; the accident of a season ... On her account, inwardly, they reproached themselves; perhaps reproached even her. If she had not married so young ... If there had been money ... This way, that way the parents turned from the disconcerting pleasure they had in her, a pleasure they felt to be stolen and not quite honourable. They had married her well, properly, formally, with a marquee; but they had not, somehow, married her *off*. She remained. But then, she was Edward's affair. In talk, Mrs Studdart again and again felt it proper to pick up Laurel's life, like a piece of unfinished sewing, and hand it back to her. Had she mislaid the pattern? Their house, on these visits, seemed to be littered with snipped muslins. They asked her about the children. .But unfortunately, when Laurel spoke of her children she became theoretic, anxious, a shade priggish. She did not see them as funny at all; she had no anecdotes. When Laurel discussed her children she bored her parents.

Mrs Studdart, never confidential to friends, had a confidante, an intimate always present, who did not exist. A lady. With her one could be certain of being understood; there prevailed a perfect good taste in which, while anything could be mentioned, too much had never been said. Someone shrewder than Willa, quicker than Mrs Bowles, with a perspective beyond Cheltenham's. In fact, a kind of sublime Mrs Studdart, with just a touch of one of the royal princesses, so that Mrs Studdart was always conscious of being seen in a large light and of arousing an agreeable interest in high quarters. This intimate was informed as to Mrs Studdart's sciatica, those qualms in the night, her mistakes at bridge, Colonel Studdart's habit of clicking his teeth while he read. She pressed Mrs Studdart's hand when a silence occurred at a dinner party. What could not be explained to her Mrs Studdart refused to recognize, what could not be described she did not observe. Any sense of guilt became a sense of complicity. Perhaps if she had been a religious woman . . . ? She wondered sometimes about Roman Catholics, whether the Virgin Mary . . .

Mrs Studdart said to her intimate: 'We both love Janet's visits, they make a point in the year. It is delightful to see her so happy and so established. She is invaluable to Rodney, the very daughter we would have wished. (When this house is gone he need not be generous any more.) As a girl, you remember, she was not always so easy. But they say the girl's marriage brings mother and daughter together; certainly nowadays there is an absolute confidence. (I could not expect her to speak of that, or that, it would not be delicate.) There is no doubt, is there, that she is satisfied? Her lovely house, all those summers and winters: perhaps a son . . .

'But Laurel makes it impossible for me to think of dying. I don't know what I am to arrange. (Oh, we enjoy her visits, we never know where we are, she makes us young!) I wish there were something else she could be, not a woman – you can't suggest? Now, of course, it is too late – and yet I can't feel everything has been quite decided. She is certainly married; I saw her myself get into the Daimler with Edward and drive off. They were so happy they never once looked round. It was an anxious day for me. "That is that," I said to myself, eleven years ago. But was it? (She is still captivating to strangers, her hair is the same colour: "Honey-colour," my husband remarked at breakfast.) What became of her? She has never been away. When this house goes – I don't know. (I told you about my heart trouble.) If Edward were ever conceivably, unkind . . . (He's devoted: they say difficult men can be so very devoted. I don't know; I've never lived with a difficult man. They have a life in London, they visit . . . they meet . . .) *I can't bear life for her!* There must be something I could arrange. You will think me foolish!'

That September the Studdarts were truly fortunate; they had both daughters with them at once. Laurel arrived two days before the end of Janet's visit. This had been Mrs Studdart's idea; she knew Janet would love to hear at first hand Laurel's still fresh account of the time in Brittany. Those two days the house beamed; doors stood open in all directions; the family reconstructed itself with talk and laughter.

On the first of these happy afternoons, Colonel Studdart walked into Cheltenham with a daughter on either arm; up the Promenade where chestnuts in the afternoon glow lifted five-fingered leaves. To left and right his friends smiled their felicitations, raising their hats; his daughters bowed smiling to left and right. The grand white pilastered house shone; the chestnuts might well have flowered. Leaves falling danced their less than moment on the gold sunshine; spring itself could not have been gayer. A touch of chill on the air made the day brighter. Along a curb, the polished cars were drawn up between white lines, diagonally: everyone was in Cheltenham. Here came the wind and a fine touch of spray: before the colonnades of the Imperial the long willow branches, the fountain blew one way, to meet the Studdarts.

They had come into Cheltenham for no reason; Colonel Studdart suggested tea. Shop windows reflected the scene and sunshine polished, a tone darker; and the three pausing figures. The tourist season was not yet over: a horn in the street, some alarm of departure brought two American visitors hurriedly down the steps of the hotel where Edward had stayed before the wedding.

Lightning Source UK Ltd.
Milton Keynes UK
UKHW022033150223
417099UK00008B/85